Mistaken Kanbans

Why The Toyota System is Not Working for You...

Mistaken Kanbans

Why The Toyota System is Not Working for You...

Yoshiki Wakai

Originally published as *Why is the Toyota Production System not working in your company? False Implementation of Kanban System*, copyright 2007 by Gijutsu-Hyohron Co., Ltd., Tokyo, Japan.

English translation © 2009 by Enna Products Corporation.

Address all comments and inquiries to:

Enna Products Corporation
1602 Carolina St.
Unit B3
Bellingham, WA 98229
Telephone: (360) 306-5369
Fax: (905) 481-0756
E-mail: info@enna.com

Printed in the United States of America

Library of Congress Control Number: 2009935909

Library of Congress Cataloging-in-Publication Data
Wakai, Yoshiki
Mistaken Kanbans
 Includes index.
 ISBN 978-1-926537-10-8
 1. Management 2. Production & Operations Managment
 3. Total Quality Management

Written by Yoshiki Wakai

English translation by Junpei Nakamuro
Illustrations by Khemanand Shiwram
Editor Collin McLoughlin
Associate Editor Shawna Gilleland

CONTENTS

Publisher's Note

I am very pleased to bring you this brilliant book, written by Mr. Yoshiki Wakai, that underlines the principles behind the Toyota Production System, and how to avoid the dilemmas that may arise while implementing this system in your company. This book, unlike other books written about the Toyota Production System and Lean Manufacturing, deals with real life issues that arise when attempting to implement the tools within the Toyota Production System. Mr. Wakai speaks from first hand experience about the practical knowledge that he has gained while being a consultant to various companies implementing the Toyota Production System.

In 1996, a revolutionary book by James P. Womack came out called *Lean Thinking - Banish Waste and Create Wealth in Your Corporation*. This book highlighted a system that provides a way for companies to be more productive and profitable by streamlining their business and utilizing a 'less is more' philosophy. This new way of thinking was predicted to bring about an era of streamlined processing and less waste. And yet, this is not the mainstream method of doing business. Why is that?

Though much has been written about the success of companies who use Lean Manufacturing and the Toyota Production System, very little has been written about the issues that can — and will — arise when implementing these systems into your company.

This book will open your eyes to the reasons why the implementation of a Kanban System, as well as other fundamental processes of Lean Manufacturing, go wrong and will assist you in understanding why. You will be led through, step by step, what is necessary to implement a successful Kanban System and how to keep negative results from arising in your company.

What most companies and managers do not realize is that the pillars behind Lean Manufacturing and the Toyota Production System, such as a Kanban System, need to be implemented company-wide, not just in a single department. For successful implementation, this also needs to be extended to a company's suppliers. After reading this book you will gain an understanding of just how important this company-wide implementation is to the overall success of the system.

Through the guidance given in this book you will be able to understand the difficulties that others have encountered and be better equipped to handle them in your own company. Not only will you be able to learn from the mistakes of others, but you will gain a better understanding of the invaluable tools that can be used to promote your company to the forefront of its industry.

What makes this book such a treasure is not only the

subject, but the nature of how it is written. The details that pervade the writing in this book, backed by decades of hands-on, real-life consulting, can help anyone increase the success of their company. No matter how great or small your knowledge of Lean Manufacturing or the Toyota Production System might be, this book will provide you with new and inspiring insights.

It is my hope that you learn from the knowledgeable lessons provided by the companies in this book and take away a greater understanding of the sub-systems that make the Kanban tool such a successful component of the Toyota Production System.

Collin McLoughlin
Publisher

FOREWORD

THE TOYOTA SYSTEM IS SIMPLE TO UNDERSTAND, BUT DIFFICULT TO PUT INTO PRACTICE

Understanding the Toyota System does not require any special knowledge. Terminologies such as "Just–in–Time," "Jidoka," and "Andon" can be easily understood with the help of many books available on the Toyota System. However, an understanding of terminologies will not lead us to a true comprehension of the underlying principles that the Toyota System is built upon.

Those who are new to the Toyota System, including many

authors from the past, have mistaken the Kanban System for the Toyota System. As a result, people have come to believe that the Toyota System is automatically implemented into production as long as Kanbans are utilized. To truly comprehend the Toyota System one must understand not only the popular terminologies, but also the fundamental principles and mechanisms behind them. This comprehensive knowledge is necessary to overcome the challenges of implementing the Toyota System successfully into production.

THE BIBLE OF THE TOYOTA SYSTEM

The bible of the Toyota System is *The Toyota Production System*, written by Taiichi Ohno (1912-1990). He learned the principles of "Just–in–Time" from the founder of Toyota Motors, Kiichiro Toyota and conceptualized its application to the real-world production system at the time. *The Toyota Production System* has been the best-selling book about the Toyota System since 1978. Taiichi Ohno's main goal of the book was to spread the principles of the Toyota System to the greater public by using simple examples with detailed explanations, so that people without manufacturing experience could grasp its concepts.

The Toyota Production System clearly illustrates the essence of the Toyota System and is a must-read for anyone who is inspired to study the Toyota System. However, in spite of the availability of this great book, people continue to misinterpret the Toyota System and suffer adverse effects on the shop floor by wrongly incorporating the Toyota System in production.

THE TOYOTA SYSTEM VOICES THE FUNDAMENTAL METHOD OF PRODUCTION

Altering existing production methods by implementing Kanbans on the shop floor without an accurate understanding of the Toyota System is likely to bring negative results to the entire production system. The Toyota System is a flow of production, and Kanbans are merely a tool to establish that flow.

Picture a production line where cars are being neatly assembled, one by one on the shop floor. That is an example of a flow in production. In Toyota, flow can be seen not only in this final stage of assembly, but also in sub-assembly lines, component fabrications, and even prior processing stages of each component on the supplier level. This flow covers every aspect of production, and is exactly what has separated Toyota from other manufacturers. To achieve such an orderly production system, it is essential that one-piece flow and diligent transportation of items happen on a continual basis. However, many factories still continue to process and transport items in batch. To overcome this habit and achieve one-piece flow, their shop floors must be constantly reexamined by continuous improvement efforts.

Continuous improvements can be achieved by first rearranging the workplace layouts and storages by practicing "Sort" and "Set in Order" methods. Overall production, especially the machinery changeover operations, needs to be continuously improved to establish a one-piece flow. Both inbound and outbound transportations, including how items are packaged, also need to be improved to ensure an efficient flow of items in production. By definition, after such improvements are made and Kanbans are applied to transfer data among processes, the Toyota System can be said to be complete. Reduced inventories, increased productivity, reduced costs, and enhanced quality standards are the end results of the Toyota System if continuous improvements are successfully carried out on a daily basis. A great deal of labor and time is necessary for adopting the Toyota System as the basic core of our manufacturing system, and must be repeatedly examined and altered. However, only spending intensive labor and time will not necessarily lead to a successful implementation of the Toyota System unless we are ready to eliminate our assumptions and accept new ideas in our thinking towards production, just like converting one's beliefs from Buddhism to Christianity, for example.

Continuous improvements without understanding the nature of the Toyota System brings out only a partial optimization of certain processes instead of an overall transformation of the entire production process, which is the most challenging aspect of the Toyota System. Therefore, understanding the Toyota System's principles is the prerequisite for establishing a successful implementation of the Toyota System.

MISTAKES ARE THE MOTHER OF SUCCESS

Learning from the successful methods of others is a shortcut to earning your own success. However, there are only a handful of companies that have succeeded in implementing the Toyota System in the past. Thus, learning their successful stories has always remained a challenge for outsiders.

In general, mistakes can be viewed as the mother of success. Even if mistakes are made it is still possible to implement the Toyota System as long as the mistakes are carefully examined and solutions are applied to overcome the problems. In other words, those without experience in the Toyota System are able to deepen their understanding of the Toyota System by learning from even the least successful examples and simulating solutions to prevent the same mistakes from reoccurring.

In this book, I will attempt to help readers strengthen their understanding towards the Toyota System by answering simple questions and providing detailed examples. The following questions are the starting point for this book:

"What are the intrinsic values of the Toyota System?"

"Why is the Toyota System not effective in your workplace?"

This book provides broad expositions on the mechanisms of the Toyota System so that new learners without prior experiences in manufacturing, can better comprehend.

I understand that most readers will have little to no experience in manufacturing or on shop floors. Many readers might have a hard time acknowledging the fact that the Toyota System is primarily a flow operation and Kanbans are just a small part of the big picture.

With such readers in mind, Chapter One illustrates various episodes concerning the realities behind pursuing the Toyota System. Chapter's Two through Five explains the reasons why the Toyota System is not effective in factories in general. Chapter Six explains various effective and proven solutions for a successful adoption of the Toyota System. The reader may stumble on some difficult concepts to understand as they read on; when that happens, just skip them and continue reading. Readers will still be able to grasp the bigger picture of what the Toyota System is all about.

Explanations found in this book do not consisted of complex terminologies or systematic interpretations of the Toyota System. It is neither designed to cover every principle within the Toyota System, nor provide detailed accounts for every continuous improvement method for you to consider. Rather, it focuses, in my own way, on showing the reality of factories attempting to adopt the Toyota System into their production system and their issues as well as effective solutions.

By the way, there are different phrases such as "the Toyota Production System" and "the Toyota System." I will use "the Toyota System" in this book.

1. Mistaken Kanbans

1-1 We Simply Misunderstood the Toyota System (my company)

The Toyota System is profitable!

Office supply manufacturer, TAIGA Office Supplies (alias), has become the top seller for IT[1] compatible office desks. The

---

1 Information Technologies - used in electronic computers and transferring electronic data. It involves personal computer hardware as well as software and fiber optics which are widely used in high speed internet network. The Japanese government started developing IT in the year 2000 as a national strategy.

current president had led the initial marketing effort and achieved tremendous success to be where he is now. Despite their larger market share, the company had several various issues to overcome. Their shop floors were far from being considered excellent, and their recent profits continued to remain lower than that of their competitors. If their factory could operate more efficiently, the production costs would decrease, resulting in a substantial profit return. The president held the factory director responsible for improving their production but yielding no promising results whatsoever.

One day, the frustrated president invited the factory director into his office and declared that his company had decided to switch over to the Toyota System due to its expected profitability. The president had been studying Toyota because they were known to be the best manufacture in Japan (Toyota recently became the top manufacture in the world[2]). As Toyota continued to expand its market share, it successfully maintained much higher revenues over its competitors. For these reasons, the president strongly believed that the Toyota System was the only answer to revitalize his own company.

The factory director, along with other shop floor workers, became panic-stricken upon learning that the Toyota System was to be adopted, as they knew that any decisions made by the president must be carried out no matter what.

> "How do we go about putting the Toyota System in place?"
>
> "Can we do it by ourselves?"

Workers were unfamiliar with the Toyota System and decided to educate themselves on principles such as "Just–in–Time," "the Kanban System" and "Jidoka" with the help of some literature. They could readily understand the terminologies and principles, however they had no idea how

2 Toyota produced more cars than General Motors in September of 2007 and became the top car manufacture in the world. Toyota is also expected to sell the most number of cars in the world.

2

to incorporate these new ideas into their daily practices as they found that the principles of the Toyota System were so unique.

After a series of serious discussions, the workers decided to give the Kanban System a try and conducted various experiments to determine if the Toyota System was actually applicable to their shop floor operations. If the Kanban System worked out, it would be great news and beneficial to their production. If it did not work out, workers simply decided to believe that the Toyota System should not have been incorporated and that the president should have just given up.

When the president explained about their strategy, he immediately told the factory director that he had found a Toyota System business consultant[3] through the CEO of Nanako Instrument and decided to have the consultant lead the process. The president was so determined that excuses were not an option.

A few weeks later, the president brought the consultant to the shop floor. After staring at the shop floor for 5 minutes, the consultant said,

> "There is no point in keeping these items around."
>
> "Find out what items are necessary or not. Eliminate unnecessary items by the next time I visit…"

Workers were busy taking notes and when they looked up, the consultant was already heading towards an exit. Workers were stunned by his bluntness but decided to follow his instruction anyway. A team dedicated to continuous improvement was organized with selected leaders from various divisions. The group focused on carrying out improvement strategies once a month while following instructions from the consultant.[4]

---

3 Business consultants who are members or alumni of the Toyota Group and provide assistance in implementing the Toyota System in factories.
4 Kaizen meetings may vary a few times per week to once per month.

Workers started by sorting out items on the shop floors. In spite of the extensive amount of labor and time required for sorting, it was rewarding for workers to see immediate results. However, as new changes were made to the production lines,[5] workers began having a hard time accepting these new changes.

> "Why do we need to adopt to different ways? Our old methods were reasonable enough... New methods may bring unwanted results... Are they really necessary?"

As the bewildered workers worried, they became unable to accept new instruction and failed to promote change any longer.

The factory director studied the progress reports with growing discomfort. "Workers are keeping themselves busy at it even though the production cost has temporarily gone up during our transition. Does that really mean that our persistent continuous improvement will finally pay off at the end?" the director repeatedly asked himself.

SUPERFICIAL ADOPTION OF THE TOYOTA SYSTEM

When workers started having doubts towards instructions given by the consultant, their continuous improvement activities began to fall behind. Workers focused on talking their way out of creating changes that they did not feel comfortable with. However, objections to the consultant were not acceptable as he was brought by the president, who also attended meetings on a regular basis. Workers eventually started to manipulate situations in order to give the impression that improvement activities were superficially[6] carried out, just to stay on the safe side.

---

5 Shop floors where components are produced from raw materials and are transported to be assembled into a product.

6 Before the consultant arrives in the shop floor, the floor layout is modified according to the consultant's instructions and is changed back after the consultant leaves the scene.

With this type of environment, you can already imagine the chaos that happened on TAIGA's shop floors. As illustrated in this case, some factories have had experiences where the Toyota System ended up being a superficial and insubstantial practice, no matter how determined ownership and management were towards adopting the Toyota System.

THE TOYOTA SYSTEM CAN BE CONFUSING SOMETIMES

Let us briefly touch on the origin of the Toyota System. Among many published books on the Toyota System, *The Toyota Production System* written by the originator of the Toyota System, Taiichi Ohno, is considered to be the bible. His book conveys that the main goal of the Toyota System is to reduce production cost by eliminating wastes. It emphasizes that such a goal can be achieved by implementing "Just–in–Time" and "Jidoka" principles.

On the other hand, the Kanban System, as a tool for the Toyota System, is relatively easy to put into practice. You have most likely heard about "Just–in–Time" and "Jidoka" if you have been studying the Toyota System at all. However, the biggest challenge that we have always faced is to gain a clear understanding of relationships between terminologies and principles themselves.

In the next section, I will illustrate a few unsuccessful stories while focusing upon two basic principles of the Toyota System: "Just–in–Time" and "Jidoka."

1-2 Reduce Inventory by "Just–in–Time"

HOW DO WE REDUCE INVENTORIES?

"Components are overflowing out of our inventories. We need to find new storage space…"
Hashimoto Precision (alias) has survived tough market com-

petition by marketing products with the use of cutting-edge technologies before their competitors. Marketing strategies of Hashimoto Precision focused on (1) introducing new products before competitors by pro actively utilizing the latest and highest quality components and (2) increasing variations in their products to meet the different needs of their customers. These strategies were inevitable for their survival, but resulted in an increased volume in inventories as a wide range of components needed to be stocked in large quantities. The production control department had tried their best to prevent overstocking with the help of spreadsheet software, but failed to control it. The reason being that new products were scheduled to launch quarterly for the next 10 years instead of once a year, as in the past.

When faced with variations in products, inventories can usually be controlled by standardizing components.[7] However, their design department was always overwhelmed with having to constantly produce new products to standardize components. In no time, their storage facilities became unable to store additional inventories for new products.

Renting more storage space was clearly not the answer for them. They had no choice but to dispose of the excess components, which eventually resulted in slowing down the entire production. Their top business administration ordered the factory to reduce the existing inventories and the shop floor workers and factory management divisions[8] made the following suggestions.

The shop floor suggested adopting the Toyota System, mainly "Just–in–Time," which would allow them to have only the necessary items at the right time, right place, and in the exact amount.

---

7 Eliminating redundancy by utilizing standardized components for different types of products and also reducing production cost by purchasing components in batch.

8 The shop floor division is a division where products are manufactured and their quality is carefully inspected. The factory management division plans and improves production as well as placing purchasing orders for necessary components.

In contrast, the factory management division suggested that ERP[9] is the only solution for eliminating any limits imposed upon production management operations.[10]

The shop floor desired to reduce inventories by reexamining the basics of manufacturing under the Toyota System which meant that continuous improvement activities would remain focused on shop floor operations. On the other hand, the factory management division aimed at reexamining production management with ERP to achieve the same goal. Installation of ERP would be carried out by the factory management division. The top business administration had to make a difficult decision between incorporating the Toyota System and ERP and finally made a decision to go with ERP.

Even though cost associated with adopting the ERP system ranges from one million to multiples of millions of dollars,[11] the business administration department thought it would be a good investment, as they expected to reduce the storage cost by eliminating inventories in a one to two year period. In fact, other companies in the same industry have been successful in incorporating ERP to yield such a result. It was also believed that the Toyota System would require too much time and labor as various other improvement activities had taken so much time on the shop floor in the past. The final decision for ERP had been made toward reducing inventories with a focus on overhauling the foundation of production management operations. At the same time, the shop floor was ordered to continue with their continuous improvement activities.

---

9 Enterprise Resource Planning is an information technology system that is designed to optimize the efficiency of various activities within a company. In a factory under an ERP, the core function lies within production management. To maintain efficient production with little or no inventory, the ordering process for both raw materials and components is carefully carried out based on the carefully planned assembly and fabrication schedules for each component.

10 Operations that oversee the entire manufacturing process including planning, purchasing, production and shipping, which are all based on incoming orders.

11 In some cases, the cost gets as high as one hundred million dollars.

A number of vendors were selling many different types of ERP systems at the time. Various aspects of production in Hashimoto Precision were carefully evaluated to select the most suitable ERP. One of the deciding factors was that "Just–in–Time" must be simulated by using ERP. The ability to have the necessary items at the right time and in the right quantity was extremely attractive to the company.

One day, an ERP system consultant[12] was invited to discuss a possible installation of ERP.

The consultant said, "This planning system[13] would allow the company to have the right component at the right time and in the right quantity. The system also performs optimized calculations for the quantity of raw materials required to produce necessary components when inventory becomes low. It will yield the same result as "Just–in–Time." This was the deciding point for Hashimoto Precision to go with this particular vendor.

After a substantial financial investment of money and one year of time trials, the system was put into full operation — reforming the entire production management.

However, the business administration observed completely opposite results than what they had expected. Their problems worsened and inventories continued to increase over time. Even the additional warehouses they had rented went over their capacity and renting more warehouses had to be considered. The investment return[14] of the ERP system was clearly questionable. ERP started to put the company in a serious financial crisis. It was supposed to have brought "Just–in–Time" into the factory. What went wrong here?

---

12 Consultants who are versed in ERP systems and give assistance in both installing and operating ERP systems.
13 A computer system that provides planning for what to buy, when to buy and how many to produce based on incoming orders.
14 Usually, a great deal of improvement can be observed in reducing both production cost and stock, which measures up to multi million dollar cost associated with adopting an ERP system in the first place.

"Just-in-Time" is considered to be one of the two fundamental principles constituting the Toyota System. It is the ideal system for having the right material at the right time, in the right place and in the right quantity.

As far as Toyota is concerned, only the necessary components arrive on the production line in the right amount, and only when needed. Thousands of unique components are assembled together to produce one automobile alone. It is quite remarkable to learn that Toyota is able to collect all the necessary components in a timely manner without any errors.

Most factories face situations where products could not be assembled due to the lack of certain components. In such a case, workers would need to hunt for missing components on a regular basis. Some factories decide to hold an excess amount of inventories to avoid a shortage of components and late deliveries of finished products to end users. Holding excess inventories also has a consequence for wasteful components if improperly allocated to accommodate the production output for any given moment. In such cases, a dramatic increase in production costs often becomes inescapable.

Problems like this are often challenged by the shop floor workers. It cannot be emphasized enough that "Just–in–Time," (having the right material at the right time, in the right place and right quantity) is the ideal solution to solve such problems.

In the case of Hashimoto Precision's factory, "Just–in–Time" would certainly have helped them reduce inventories if properly put into practice. However, they experienced an increase in stock that can be explained by reasons like incorrect programming of ERP, the inability to comply with ERP instructions, or some other reason that they were not yet aware of.

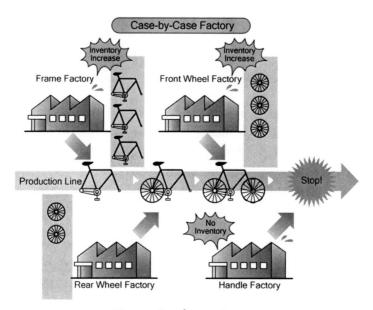

Figure 1: *Case-by-case Factory*

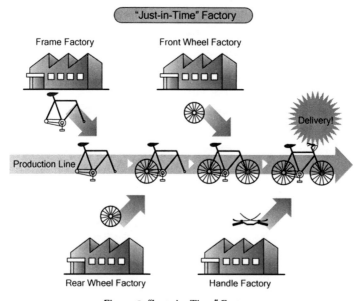

Figure 2: *"Just-in-Time" Factory*

As a matter of fact, the ERP consultant misinterpreted the true meaning of "Just–in–Time" (JIT). JIT must start from accomplishing continuous improvement on the shop floor as a prerequisite.[15] On the other hand, ERP was able to provide only a theorized JIT that may not yield desired results in practice. The desired result of JIT is only attainable when its meaning and application are clearly understood.

In the next section, I will illustrate examples in which "Elimination of Wastes", another fundamental concept of the Toyota System, was unsuccessful in practice.

1-3 Never-ending 5S and Waste Elimination

5S AS THE FOUNDATION FOR IMPROVING THE SHOP FLOOR

The Sakura Factory (alias) offers product assembly services to a well-known electric equipment manufacturer. They have been unsuccessful in reducing the price of their services as requested by their client. They recently suffered from tough market competition against Chinese factories and faced a serious risk of losing business. In the past, they have outsourced their production to less costly factories[16] to lower their prices. Now, a much more effective solution was needed to meet their client's harsher demands.

The Sakura Factory tried various continuous improvement methods to reduce their production costs without any satisfactory progress. In spite of their well-established plans and goals at the beginning, they neglected to include themselves in some aspects of improvement activities, as it was a

---

15 If components do not arrive in a timely manner by "Just–in–Time", effective solutions will be carefully formulated by a series of continuous improvement activities on the shop floor.

16 Reducing the production cost by hiring other factories to perform the required processing with their lower labor costs.

company-driven effort. To overcome this shortcoming, they decided to hire a non-company affiliated consultant to help them boost their efforts toward improving production.

At first, they had no idea where to look for a consultant who specialized in continuous improvement. They started by searching online by using keywords such as, "the Toyota System", "cost-down" and "consultants." They gathered a list of candidates and conducted interviews with each consultant. The final candidate was selected based on his personality and the fact that he could commit long-term to their company.

The first day on the shop floor, the consultant expressed that the key to success in continuous improvement was the 5S[17] solution. His strategy was to remove wastes by 5S and eventually gain a needed reduction in production costs.

5S slogans have been present in the Sakura Factory for a long time. Despite this, they have always had a difficult time finding where necessary items were located in their overcrowded shop floors. 5S had never been implemented in spite of their slogans.

The consultant gave out instructions to pick out only the necessary items and throw away the rest. Workers were hesitant to throw away items that could still be used. But, with the use of red tags, they eventually had the courage to do so. As the factory gradually became arranged, wastes became more apparent and were removed from the shop floor.

The consultant gave out another instruction to incorporate the "7 Wastes" principle in an attempt to take improvements on the shop floor to the next level. This allowed workers to eliminate wastes that they had been unable to identify in the past. However, in some cases, a certain degree of hesitation among workers was evident as removing wastes required rearranging the shop floor layout and changing their work methods for various operations, including transporting fin-

17 5S is consisted of Sorting, Set in Order, Sweeping, Standardizing and Sustaining.

ished products.

Such hesitations were overcome by the consultant's assurance that everything could be put back into the original state if no improvement was achieved. He also stressed that doing nothing about it was the worst thing workers could have done. Successful elimination of wastes continued to take place as a result.

After one year the factory had become drastically standardized. The factory director looked forward to hearing how much the production costs had been reduced by improvement activities and increasing the labor efficiency of each worker on the shop floor.[18]

> "Production costs have been reduced only this much?"

The factory director finally studied the report and was disappointed with the results. He had expected a larger reduction in production costs. Unfortunately, their continuous improvement effort over a period of one year was simply not sufficient for surviving through the tough competition with the Chinese market.

5S AND THE TOYOTA SYSTEM

Unnecessary items are being stored somewhere and workers have a hard time locating items when they become necessary. Over time, you will discover old clothes stored in your closet that no longer fit. Either you cannot seem to throw them away or you simply do not want them to go to waste.

Have you had a similar experience in the past?

Factories today are experiencing a very similar situation. When you walk into a factory, you will notice posters and banners that are designed to constantly remind workers of

---

18 When a worker only takes 6 hours to perform a certain task instead of 12 hours as he did in the past, his labor efficiency increases by 50%.

the 5S principles. The 5S principles are as follows:

Seiri (Sorting) - Practice of keeping only essential items and removing the unessential items.

Seiton (Set in Order) - Tools and materials are arranged to allow easy access.

Seisou (Sweeping) - Keep the workplace orderly to maintain productivity.

Seiketsu (Standardizing) - Standardize the workplace by Sorting, Set in Order and Sweeping.

Shitsuke (Sustaining) – Follow standards and rules.

Terminologies such as 2S and 4S[19] also exist depending on how many principles are taken into consideration.

5S is the fundamental requirement for the shop floor and is practiced in many factories. 5S is known to boost the efficiency in operation and expose problems before they become serious. 5S also promotes cleanliness in the work place and leads to enhanced work ethics of workers on the shop floor.

WHAT ARE THE 7 TYPES OF WASTES?

Thorough elimination of wastes is the basic principle of the Toyota System. Wastes can be divided into 7 categories as follows:

1. Over-production
2. Waiting
3. Transporting

19 The 2S's consists of Sorting and Set in Order. The 4S's consists of Sorting, Set in Order, Sweeping and Standardizing. Some organizations have added a 5th S, Sustain.

4. Processing
5. Inventory
6. Motion
7. Defects

These wastes exist in abundance in factories around the world. If you train your eyes to look around a little bit deeper, you will discover a new array of wastes in your work place. Execution of the 5S's is essentially a waste removal activity as it focuses on removing unnecessary items.

SORTING IS THE BASIC ORGANIZATION PRINCIPLE

Using red tags is proven to be an effective way to reduce wastes. This is what the Sakura Factory decided to incorporate into their continuous improvement activities. Red tags are applied to items that may not be useful anymore and are gathered in one location. When any of the items become necessary, the red tags are removed and items are taken out of the pile. If an item has retained a red tag after a significant amount of time that item will be removed permanently.

The same technique can be applied to a household environment, for example. Red tags are put on every hanger that holds your suits. As you take a suit out to wear, the red tag is removed. Suits left with red tags will be thrown away after a year or so.

NEVER-ENDING 5S AND WASTE ELIMINATION

5S and Waste Elimination are extremely important principles to exercise. However, positive results can never be substantial if they are practiced for only a short period of time.

In the beginning, the Sakura Factory observed their work place environment improve rapidly as a result of their 5S and waste removal efforts. Over time, as they continued their efforts, they started to focus on meeting only the goals of the 5S and waste removal, instead of targeting at reducing production costs on a large scale.

Many factories are experiencing the same situation where workers become content only with the outcome of their 5S activities or feel the limitations of 5S leaving them no clues as to what to try next.

In the next section, I will illustrate some examples where factories failed in incorporating the Kanban System.

1-4 Defeated by the Kanban System

THE KANBAN SYSTEM GIVES US HOPE

Nishimura Machinery (alias) sells production equipment that is manufactured in their factory. Nishimura has experienced an increased number of orders from overseas, especially from China, and had a hard time keeping up with the demand. They had to spend most of their improvement efforts on maintaining their large inventory to avoid shortages, which was the primary reason why they had fallen behind their production quota.

Necessary components were either produced in their own factories or were purchased from suppliers. Problems existed in both cases. In-house components were manufactured at the convenience of their processing plant and were transported to the assembly plant in batch. Most of the transported components ended up being in storage for so long that they became too degraded to be used in production. In some cases particular components failed to arrive in time, which often required factory leaders to go out of their way to retrieve them from the processing plant.

On the other hand, the delivery of components from suppliers often took more than a month[20] for delivery. For this reason, components needed to be pre-ordered well in advance. Even after components were ordered, the purchasing department was often preoccupied with making last minute changes to their orders. In addition, not all of the suppliers were able to deliver components in time. They needed to call suppliers every day to make sure that everything was on schedule.

The Nishimura factory decided to implement the Kanban System as a solution to their problems after the chief production manager toured their parent factory and discovered that inventory management costs could be significantly reduced by the Toyota System.

In the beginning, the Kanban System was introduced to their own processing plants. Production of exterior components[21] was prioritized as they had to be manufactured the most frequently and therefore, consumed the most storage space. If the Kanban System turned out to be effective, they could certainly expect to reduce inventories and storage space by having the right components at the right time and in the right quantity every time.

A Kanban was placed on each package that indicated how many exterior components needed to be packed inside. The Kanbans also designated a location where the package needed to be stored within the factory. Their processing department was instructed to follow such Kanbans diligently. Some workers had a difficult time dealing with Kanbans in the beginning but managed to integrate Kanbans into their work routine without any issues.

---

20 If a component is available in stock, suppliers ask for only a few days to deliver the component. However, if it is a customized or build-to-order component, suppliers ask for more than a month for delivery.
21 The type of components that can be seen on the outside of a product such as a plastic enclosure of computers.

Inventories of exterior components were drastically reduced as they were transported to the assembly plant in the quantity specified by Kanbans. The production chief observed this positive outcome of Kanbans and decided to expand its use to maintaining other components including those from their suppliers.

After one year had passed since Kanbans were put into practice, a manager from the parent company was invited to evaluate what had been accomplished in the Nishimura factory.

The manager asked the production chief, "How are things in your factory with the Kanban System?"

The production chief replied, "It has been a challenging year for us but everything seems to run smoothly these days and we are focused on expanding the use of Kanbans in our production."

As they continued to tour the factory, the manager asked another question, "How many components do these packages contain anyway?"

The production chief was surprised to receive such a question. He thought that the manager, an expert at dealing with Kanbans, should be able to answer his own question by simply looking at the Kanban.

The manger asked another question, "The quantity specified on the Kanban does not match the quantity in the package, does it?"

The production chief looked at the package and, sure enough, found only 4 components, one component short of the quantity indicated by the Kanban.

"By the way, how many days of production do these components supply for? I think it is a bit too much[22]."

As a matter of fact, these components were pre-ordered and stored for two weeks of production, which was actually worse than the situation that they had experienced before. The production chief went to the purchasing department to find out what had gone wrong with their Kanban System. Apparently, their suppliers demanded to raise the price of components due to their increased expenses associated with frequent delivery trips. The production chief became completely lost in finding an effective solution to battle this situation.

KANBANS ARE JUST A WASTE OF PAPER

There is no point in keeping the Kanban System when inventories continue growing to a point where there is no room left to store the necessary items. Many factories experience this completely opposite result. What have they done wrong to draw such a negative outcome? If no action is taken to remedy the situation, Kanbans just end up being a waste of paper and we will keep going back to the same problems over and over.

THE SUPERMARKET AND THE KANBAN SYSTEM

The Kanban System derived its fundamental ideas from supermarkets in the United States of America. As you already know, necessary items can be purchased at any time in the quantity you desire from supermarkets. Kanbans allows factories to purchase components in the same way to prepare for daily production. If an item is sold and taken off of the inventory, the supermarket will order that item before a customer looks for it.

---

22 It is considered a sign of improvement to be able to determine what is being excessive or not on the shop floor as it was nearly impossible to do so in the past.

Supermarkets inform the preceding processes[23] in the factory or suppliers of what items they need in what quantity and when by utilizing a schedule system called the Kanban System. Kanbans are divided into two categories: Retrieval Kanban and Instruction Kanban.

> **Parts Withdrawal Kanban** – Instruction as to how many items need be transported.

> **Production Instruction Kanban** – Instruction as to how many items need to be produced.

Parts Withdrawal Kanbans are used when a preceding process has components ready to go. On the other hand, Production Instruction Kanbans are used when a preceding process produces components on demand.

For example, Japanese bookstores utilize a similar system for ordering books using order tags. Each book has a colored tag inside with its title written on it. If a book is sold, the tag is removed and sent to a supplier so that it can be reordered. This system allows bookstores to circulate their inventories and make sure every book is in stock at all times.

I have talked about examples in which adoption of the Toyota System was unsuccessful. In the next section, I will analyze the reasons why.

---

23 "Processes" signify the order of production. When a component flows from the processing department to an assembly department, the processing department is the "preceding process" of assembly department and assembly department is the "post-process" of processing department respectively. In a larger perspective, a purchasing department is the "proceeding process" and marketing activities or end-users can be considered as the "post-processes" in factory settings.

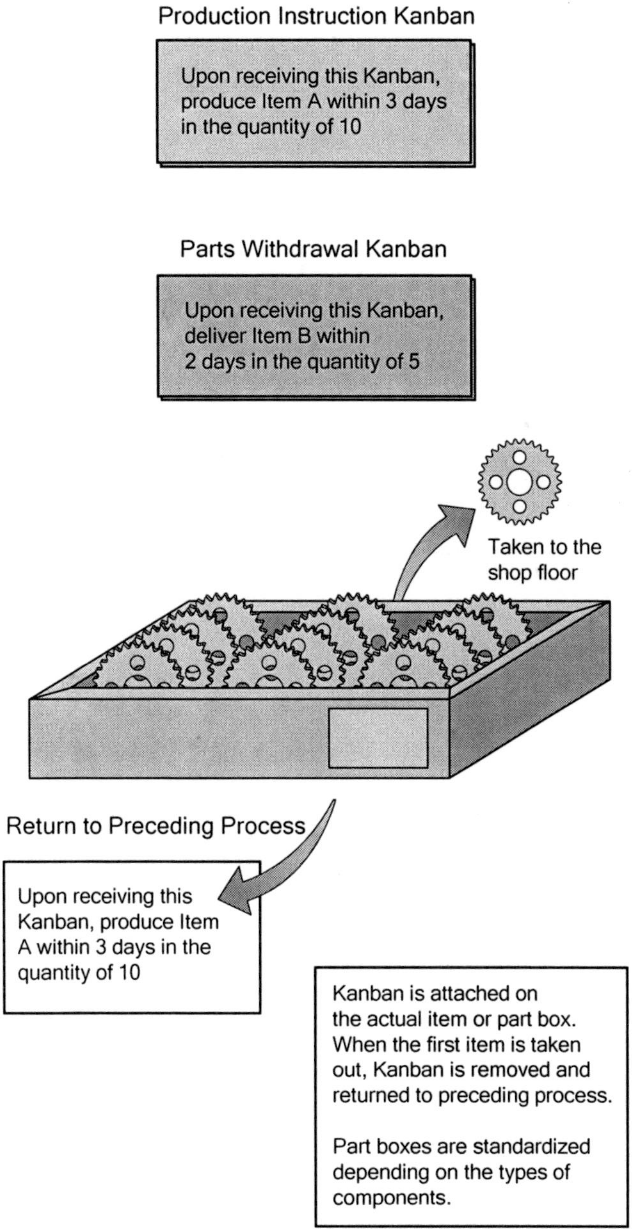

Production Instruction Kanban

> Upon receiving this Kanban, produce Item A within 3 days in the quantity of 10

Parts Withdrawal Kanban

> Upon receiving this Kanban, deliver Item B within 2 days in the quantity of 5

Taken to the shop floor

Return to Preceding Process

> Upon receiving this Kanban, produce Item A within 3 days in the quantity of 10

Kanban is attached on the actual item or part box. When the first item is taken out, Kanban is removed and returned to preceding process.

Part boxes are standardized depending on the types of components.

Figure 3: Production Instruction & Parts Withdrawal Kanbans

2. The Real Explanation of the Toyota System

2-1 Waste Elimination is the Foundation of the Toyota System

All everyone talks about is Kanbans

When someone mentions that their company started incorporating the Kanban System, almost everyone in the manufacturing business knows what they are talking about.

"Is it going well? It's a challenge isn't it?" would be typical responses from workers in a factory where the Kanban System is being introduced for the first time as well.

"Was the Kanban System implemented because your customer insisted on it? It's a challenge isn't it? " would be typical responses from suppliers.

Most workers are also likely to respond, "The Kanban System... You must have started transitioning towards the Toyota System."

Many people tend to think that adoption of the Kanban System automatically means that the Toyota System is in place. This is simply not true. The Kanban System is only a tool that helps the Toyota System operate in the way it is supposed to. Without the Toyota System, the Kanban System simply ceases to exist.

In addition, the Kanban System has been misinterpreted by many factories to a point where its true purpose is ignored. Let us reflect on the origin of the Toyota System so that we are no longer confused.

DESIRES TO INCREASE PRODUCTIVITY AND REDUCE PRODUCTION COST HAVE CREATED "JUST–IN–TIME"

The basic philosophy of the Toyota System relies on the absolute elimination of wastes. It must be noted that cost reduction is the true goal of waste elimination, not merely removing wastes around us.

After World War II, the productivity of Japanese factories recorded only 12% of that of American factories. This big difference was explained by the wasteful production methods found in Japanese factories. The Toyota System was essentially designed to boost the productivity of Japanese factories in order to compete with American industry.

In the past, Toyota was unable to complete their work due to shortages of components in the first half of the month. Therefore, it forced them to complete their work in the later half of the month, after all the necessary components were delivered to the shop floor. That was the obvious reason for their low productivity.

24

To battle this inefficiency, Toyota decided to change its method completely. Instead of finishing their necessary work with 100 workers towards the end of a month, they determined the average workload that must be completed on a daily basis. In this manner, they were able to boost their overall productivity and completed the work with only 50 workers.

Every necessary component needed to arrive in the factory in a timely manner to ensure that the average workload gets completed. They needed to avoid overstocking components, as it would cause cost increases, in case products did not sell as planned.

With that in mind, Taiichi Ohno from Toyota Industry formulated the ideal way of production, a "flow" in which necessary components arrived in the factory in the right quantity and time, and all of the finished products were shipped out daily. To achieve such a flow, he conceptualized "Just-in-Time" and its wide range of applications.

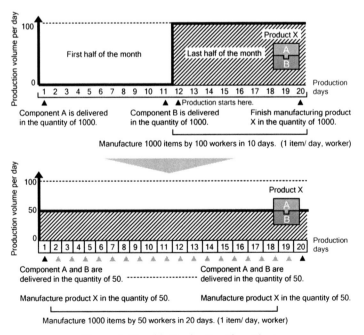

Figure 4: Monthly Production Flow Charts

KANBANS ARE A METHOD FOR TRANSFERRING INFORMATION

The Toyota System is essentially a method that advocates an ideal system of production. Kanbans are only a tool to promote such an ideal production system.

The Toyota System creates a flow in production. To achieve a flow, the Kanban System is often utilized as a mode for transferring important data. If a flow cannot be achieved in production it means that the Kanban System is not practiced effectively, putting an end to adopting The Toyota System.

"JUST–IN–TIME" AND "JIDOKA" ARE THE PILLARS OF THE TOYOTA SYSTEM

The Toyota System has been developed since the 1940's as an ideal method for producing a wide variety of products in small quantities with low production costs. The goal of the Toyota System is not to mass produce items to lower their costs. It focuses on deriving every workers' potential, creating a great working environment, and providing customers with affordable items, which are made possible by absolute elimination of wastes and maximizing available capital resources.

"Just–in–Time" and "Jidoka"[1] are the backbones for accomplishing absolute elimination of wastes.

"Just–in–Time" can be realized in the following steps:

- Post-processes transfer data to preceding processes using Kanbans.
- Post-processes retrieve items from preceding processes at the right time and in the right quantity.
- Preceding processes produce only the number of items that has been taken away from post-process.

---

1 Jidoka is originally formulated by Sakichi Toyota, the company founder of Toyota, who invented mistake-proof devices to be incorporated in weaving machines.

"Jidoka" can be realized in following these steps:

- Allow the shop floor workers and their machinery to perform supervisory functions over producing only what is qualified to be good products. If a defect occurs, automation is stopped by various mistake-proof mechanisms.
- The main objectives are eliminating defects and preventing overproduction from occurring.

How to Eliminate Wastes

As mentioned above, the basic philosophy of the Toyota System relies on the absolute elimination of wastes. If wastes are removed completely from a workplace, a flow in production will start to formulate. However, paying too much attention only to smaller wastes poses a risk of leaving larger wastes unidentified.

In many factories waste removal activities are performed with full participation from workers in small groups while following the instructions from supervisors on the shop floor. However, workers are often fixated on removing wastes found only in their own behaviors and work cells. For this reason, workers ignore removing wastes in the context of a flow such as looking at every process involved in purchasing through delivery of finished products. Consequently, their effort would become a waste itself if production methods were to be changed in any way.

I cannot stress enough that both 5S and Waste Elimination are indispensable continuous improvement activities. However, it takes more than these activities to achieve the ideology put forth by The Toyota System. If only the 5S's and Waste Elimination efforts were put into practice repeatedly it would require more time and trials (if not equal to) than what Toyota has taken to achieve the goal.

2-2 Basic Principles of "Just–in–Time", the Foundation for Removing Wastes

KANBANS MAKE "JUST–IN–TIME" COME TRUE

There are two main effective methods for applying "Just–in–Time." One method is to carry no inventories and order either a preceding process, or a supplier to deliver the necessary items within a few hours to one day. This is literally a "Just–in–Time" activity and is also referred to as "Sequential Parts Withdrawal," an ideal method for avoiding the risk of overstocking items.

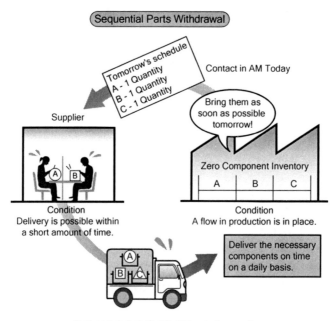

Deliver Ax1, Bx1, Cx1 first thing in the morning.

Figure 5: Sequential Parts Withdrawal

However, this can only be achieved by working closely with preceding processes or suppliers that are capable of providing items in such a short time. Periodical delays or inaccurate supplies of items are never allowed, for which a great deal of commitments and the capacity to follow orders are required, to say the least.

The other method is for a post-process to maintain a bare minimum of stock. In this method, if stocked items are used up, the exact number of items are ordered from a preceding process or a supplier. When an item is needed for production, it is taken out of stock and is reordered from a supplier for the next time it is needed. In this method, the necessary items are always available in the right quantities by adjusting the existing inventory. This method no longer needs to take into consideration the time required to deliver each component to the shop floor. Kanbans can be used for reporting necessary items and their quantity to a preceding process or a supplier. This is called the "Kanban System."

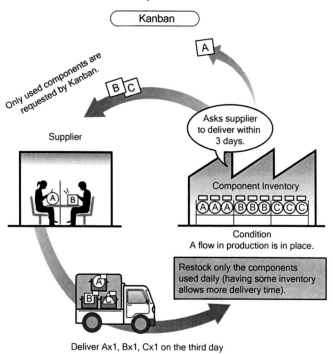

Figure 6: Kanban Parts Withdrawal

Therefore, "Just–in–Time" with the use of Kanbans has the precondition of having the minimum amount of stock sufficient for production rather than focusing on maintaining zero-stock.

"Just–in–Time" derives its basic ideas from the supermarkets we see in our daily lives. Examining how supermarkets operate allows you to gain a clear understanding of "Just–in–Time." Supermarkets are located in convenient locations and carry various essential items at reasonable costs. They have become indispensable establishments for our everyday living. Providing customers with an environment where "necessary groceries can be purchased in the right quantity at the right amount," supermarkets are essentially a "Just–in–Time" System. We tend to take supermarkets for granted. But, studying the mechanisms of supermarkets allows us to learn preconditions that need to be met for success.

SUPERMARKETS ALWAYS CARRY "WHAT YOU NEED"

Supermarkets have always attracted consumers as everything from meat to fish to spices can be bought at the same location. In the past, customers needed to go to separate stores to buy those items. Supermarkets were able to save customers time and effort by carrying everything that any customer wanted under the same roof. This is the very reason that has made supermarkets indispensable to our lives.

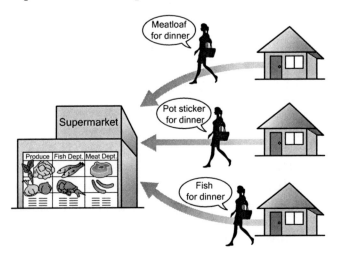

Figure 7: Benefits of Supermarkets

The key to their success is stocking every item at any given time. However, supermarkets need to guarantee an environment where customers can easily find what they need, even if the volume of stock items increases. Every shelf also needs to be clearly labeled and the floor layout needs to be carefully designed so that customers can find their items without difficulty. Repeat customers are able to complete their shopping in a short amount of time as item locations hardly change. In any event, supermarkets lose their importance if they fail to provide customers with what they really need and want.

SUPERMARKETS "ALWAYS" CARRY ITEMS YOU NEED

Another appealing aspect of supermarkets is that they always have the items you need in stock. To enable customers to purchase at their convenience items need to be displayed on shelves at any given time. If an item is sold and the shelf is not restocked customers will not be able to purchase the item and supermarkets will lose their customers. That is why supermarkets stock a certain number of items in their storage and refill the shelves by adjusting the inventories, which enables them to have items on the shelves at all times.

SUPERMARKETS CARRY ITEMS ONLY IN THE NECESSARY QUANTITY

Supermarkets need to pay more attention to the most popular items that are sold in large quantities. As I mentioned before, delaying restocking shelves poses a serious risk of losing customers. On the other hand, sustaining a large volume of inventories leads to issues with unsold items and display space being wasted. Most food items have expiration dates, which require supermarkets to destroy such items[2] if not sold. Destroying unsold food items is not only a waste in ordering but also a waste in human labor in getting rid of such items. These types of wastes must be eliminated to avoid

2 Remaining perishable items are sold off at discounted prices as high as 50% off the original prices prior to the store closing time in order to avoid waste.

price increases and reductions in profit. Supermarkets battle this issue by stocking up on items that are sold daily from suppliers as soon as they possibly can to avoid shortage of items in their inventory.

SALES FORECAST OF SUPERMARKETS

It is equally important for supermarkets to forecast their daily sales. Even though every household has a different dinner menu, certain grocery items are sold at predictable ratios in a large perspective. There are never cases where "only" the groceries for meatloaf or pot stickers are sold in a given day. However, relative quantities of sold groceries, a ratio between groceries for meatloaf and pot stickers, is attainable on a daily basis.

By utilizing such data effectively it is possible for supermarkets to predict a daily sales volume and calculate the right amount of stock to be displayed — without experiencing shortages at any given time.

However, nothing is perfect. If a certain item gets sold unexpectedly, supermarkets will experience a shortage due to insufficient stock to accommodate it. There is also a risk in overstocking of unpopular items at the same time.

For an example, when Natto (fermented soy beans, a popular Japanese ingredient) is reported to be very healthy on TV, sales for Natto will be likely to drastically increase, which may disable regular Natto consumers to purchase the amount they usually need. In addition, when certain customers decide to stock up on certain items many stores may fail to sell such items to regular customers. This kind of situation was observed when people stocked up on toilet paper[3] during the oil shocks of the 1970s. With these exceptions, supermarkets provide customers with a stable shopping environment

---

3 The oil crisis in 1973 began as the result of the Yom Kippur War. The price of gas had skyrocketed causing the prices of oil-related items to increase significantly. People stocked up on toilet paper to avoid potential shortages.

where they can purchase any items at any time.

HOW TO SUCCESSFULLY IMPLEMENT "JUST–IN–TIME" IN SUPERMARKETS

A supermarket has to have the following preconditions: a wide range of items need to be available with a constant rate of sales, it also has to stock items to avoid shortages and continues to restock inventory as items are being sold.

As for buyers, it is preconditioned that buyers purchase items at a frequent rate without concentrating on buying certain items.

As for supermarkets, it is preconditioned that:

- Items can be delivered immediately after they are sold off the shelf.
- Items can be purchased and restocked by the supplier for the exact quantity sold.
- Items can be restocked on a daily basis.

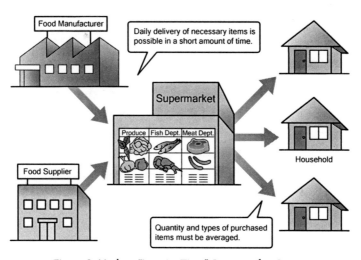

Figure 8: Modern "Just–in–Time" Supermarket System

It is true that buying trends among consumers are unpredictable, but unless some irregular buying trends occur, every item is sold almost equally across the board. In the past designated wholesale stores have performed the role of maintaining a flow of items among supermarkets in Japan. In recent years, supermarkets have a network with other super-markets so that a smooth logistic of items can be established to achieve an effective "Just–in–Time" System.

How to successfully implement "Just–in–Time" in factories

Requirements for a successful implementation of "Just–in–Time" in supermarkets also applies to factories. To supply components under a "Just–in–Time" System requires assembly lines and component suppliers to do the following:

Assembly lines are required to:

- Average production[4] and avoid batch production.

Preceding process or suppliers are required to:

- Supply only the required components in a short amount of time.
- Supply components only in the required amount for production.
- Supply components on a daily basis.

In factories, it is also important for a production line to average both the amount and the types of items to be produced on a daily basis. In addition, preceding process and suppliers need to produce and transport requested components diligently at every level.

---

4 Avoid inconsistency in production pertaining not only to the quantities, but also to the kind of items.

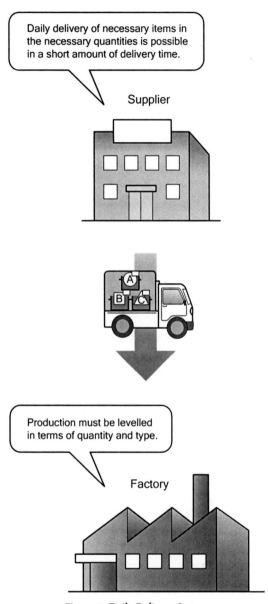

Figure 9: Daily Delivery System

A significant reduction in inventory can be accomplished by a successful adoption of the Toyota System. However, some factories have misunderstood that the Toyota System automatically leads to a zero-inventory system.

I would like to share my experience with you here. I came across a true or false question in an examination which asked, "The Toyota System is a method for achieving a zero-inventory system." I marked "false" with confidence, but was wrong in my judgment when I received my results later on.

As I illustrated before, "Sequential Parts Withdrawal," a method in which suppliers deliver components instantly upon requests, is designed to promote a zero-inventory system without using Kanbans.

However, a flow in production with assistance from well-qualified suppliers capable of supplying parts on demand is a precondition for sustaining a "Sequential Parts Withdrawal" System. Otherwise, suppliers would be burdened by having to hold their own inventory so that you can completely remove inventory from your own factory.

To incorporate "Just–in–Time" in practice correctly, factories should hold a certain volume of inventory in their own facilities and use Kanbans to instruct suppliers to deliver necessary components. At the same time, factories need to focus on creating a flow in production, which will eventually help them reduce inventory close to zero while maximizing potentials of their suppliers.

2-3 Basic Principle in Eliminating Wastes by Implementation of "Jidoka"

"Jidoka" is the other fundamental principle in the Toyota System besides "Just–in–Time." Toyota's slogan, "Thorough Elimination of Wastes," signifies "overproduction" to be the most problematic type of waste. "Jidoka" is designed to prevent this overproduction and defects from occurring in production.

First, let us examine the Japanese characters for Jidoka, 自働化. Jidoka is made up of three letters; 自 'self', 働 'movement' and 化 '-ization'. The letter 働 for 'movement' is a character derived by adding a radical representing 'human', which signifies transferring human intelligence to machines instead of using them as just machines.

This "Jidoka" was also formulated after having overcome various challenges. During a high-growth period in the 70's, the main goal of Japanese factories was to mass-produce items to keep up with the growing market demand. To achieve this goal, high-tech machines designed to complete processes in a short time by automation were needed, but they were extremely costly for most factories to purchase. Factories had no choice but conduct a higher-volume manufacturing to pay off costs associated with buying such machines. However, a large amount of defects were produced as a result of mass production when machines failed to perform as expected. Some factories went as far as designating workers to supervise machines at all times to avoid serious damages to machines themselves. Their efforts consequently increased the overall cost and made it pointless to include such expensive machines into production.

To battle these situations, machines were given devices

designed to stop automation when machines themselves made judgments as to what went right or wrong. "Jidoka" is essentially giving machines human intelligence and an ability to make judgments.

"POKA-YOKE" IS AN INTELLIGENCE GIVEN TO MACHINES

"Poka-yoke" devices signify a form of intelligence given to machines and tools used in manufacturing. If we look up the word, "poka-yoke" in a Japanese dictionary, you will find its definition as "an unexpected bad hand in a game of Japanese chess or GO." In the same sense, "poka-yoke" are designed to prevent such unthinkable mistakes from occurring in the first place.

For example, when a worker makes defects by not inserting a component in the correct orientation, such defects can be prevented by installing pins so that the component can only be installed in the correct way. In other words, if inserted in a wrong position, a worker becomes unable to continue to do his work. The point is to develop simple mistake-proofing devices that are extremely effective and inexpensive. In recent years, various "poka-yoke" devices have been developed and put into practice in many production lines.

PREVENTING OVERPRODUCTION BY THE "FULL WORK SYSTEM"

"Jidoka" prevents factories not only from producing defects but also from overproducing. A "Full Work System" is designed to remove overproduction from various manufacturing processes.

Troubles are inevitable when it comes to manufacturing. When a certain machine breaks down in a production line, its preceding process would need to stop its operation to avoid an overflow of items being produced.

To overcome this process, overproduction can be avoided

by specifying work tables where finished items are stored in certain quantities. When work tables run out of space, it signifies production to stop at once. When space becomes available as items are used in productions, it signifies production to start. This type of system is classified as the "Full Work System."

This "Full Work System" in partnership with Kanbans plays a very important role in conducting flow manufacturing on a large scale.

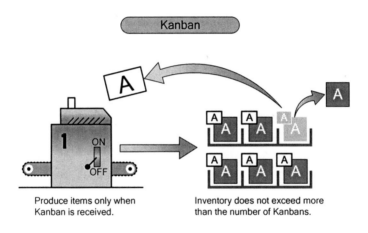

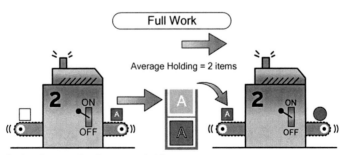

Figure 10: Kanban vs. Full Work System

3. I Knew that Kanbans were Important

3-1 The Fundamentals of Kanbans

Kanbans indicate how products should be manufactured

Various items travel through a factory having transformed from raw materials into components, then from components into finished products at a final stage. Let us follow this path and examine each part of the entire process.

At the very beginning, raw materials are purchased from suppliers and are transported into designated storage spaces. Stored materials are then transported to a machining facility and wait for their turns to be processed into components. Finished components are stored near a machining facility for a period of time and are transported into storage spaces for finished components. Components are then transported to a production line and wait for their turn to be used in an assembly. Assembled products are kept near a production line for awhile and are transported to storage spaces as finished products. Finished products are then shipped out of storage spaces as purchase orders come in.

The production control department in a factory usually designs a "Planned Manufacturing System" that suggests and maintains a flow in various production processes. Instructions are given to every process as to "When," "What," "Where" and "How many" each item should be produced as well as "Where" finished items should be transported to and from.

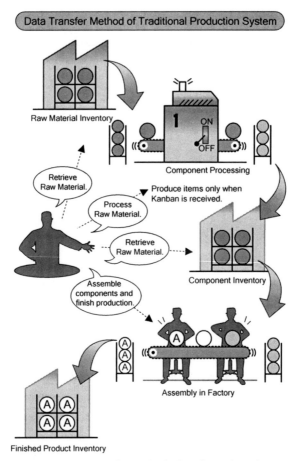

Figure II: Data Transfer Method of Traditional Production

On the other hand, in the Toyota System, a certain amount of inventory (raw materials, components and so on) is sustained in places like machining facilities, assembly lines and component storages and is distributed by utilizing Kanbans in the following ways:

- Transport components back to an assembly line from component storage after they are used for assembly (Inter-Process Kanban).
- Machining facilities produce components only in the quantity that they were transported to the assembly line from the component storage.

In short, Kanbans are used by post-processes to instruct preceding processes as to "What" component needs to be transported as well as exactly "When," "How" and "To Where" (Production Instruction Kanban).

Kanbans are attached on each component beforehand and are removed when components become used. Removed Kanbans are then sent back to a preceding process. The shop floor workers in charge of a machining facility are instructed to produce and transport the necessary components according to what Kanbans indicate. In such cases, Kanbans transfer such data from post-processes to preceding process. Workers should produce or deliver as follows:

What — as indicated by Kanban

How many — as indicated by Kanban

When — as indicated by Kanban

To Where — as indicated by Kanban

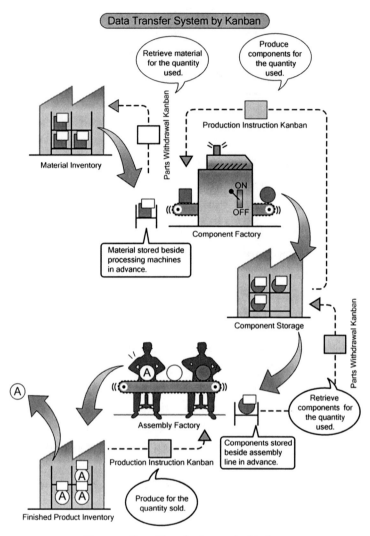

Figure 12: Data Transfer System by Kanban

SIX RULES OF KANBANS

The following rules must be followed to operate productions under Kanbans:

> *Rule 1*
>
> As indicated by Kanbans that were removed from items, post-process retrieves only the necessary items in the necessary quantities from a preceding process (Kanbans function as "Withdrawal

Data" and "Transportation Instruction Data").

Rule 2

Preceding process produces the necessary items on the order as indicated by Kanbans (Kanbans function as "Production Instruction Data").

Rule 3

Unless Kanbans are removed, post-processes do not retrieve any items from preceding processes. In the same respect, preceding processes do not produce items unless they are instructed to do so by Kanbans (Kanbans function as a way of preventing overproduction and over-transportation).

Rule 4

Kanbans must be attached to the actual items at all times. Kanbans can be considered identification tags (items with accompanying Kanbans are considered as necessary items for production).

Rule 5

Items to which Kanbans can be applied must be free of defects (when a defect occurs, the responsible process must immediately prevent it from reoccurring in the future).

Rule 6

Gradually reduce the number of Kanbans being used (Kanbans are tools for exposing problems on the surface, the shop floor must be continuously improved to solve such problems).

Without following these important rules described above, factories will not only experience unsatisfactory results but also may impose adverse effects beyond their own factories. I will explain such adverse effects later in the book.

3-2 Let's make a Kanban

RECIPE FOR CREATING A PRACTICAL KANBAN

In this section, I will demonstrate how to make a Kanban that can be put into practice. A Kanban can be easily made by anyone with a pen and a piece of paper. Please refer to the instruction figure below.

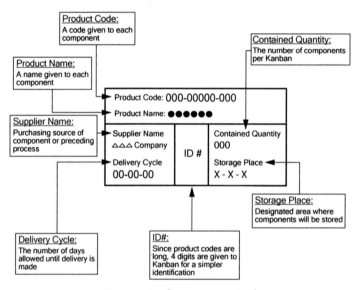

Figure 13: Kanban Equation Card

It is relatively easy, is it not? We need to figure out next how many Kanbans should be prepared.

DETERMINING HOW MANY KANBANS TO BE PREPARED

Kanbans must be attached to actual items as a general rule. The number of Kanbans decides the volume of inventory to be maintained. It means that a factory could suffer from an excess amount of inventory or a shortage in necessary items if the number of Kanbans is not appropriately calculated in advance. In practice, it remains a challenge to determine an appropriate number of Kanbans. But, the equations illustrated below can help us calculate it.

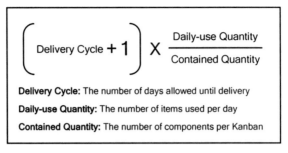

$$\left(\text{Delivery Cycle} + 1 \right) \times \frac{\text{Daily-use Quantity}}{\text{Contained Quantity}}$$

Delivery Cycle: The number of days allowed until delivery

Daily-use Quantity: The number of items used per day

Contained Quantity: The number of components per Kanban

Figure 14: Kanban Equation

QUANTITY AS INDICATED BY KANBANS, "CONTAINED QUANTITY"

The equations consist of 3 factors such as "Contained Quantity," "Delivery Cycle" and "Daily-use Quantity." Let me explain these factors.

The quantity written in a Kanban is called "Contained Quantity." That tells us how many items to be prepared for.

If we strictly follow the rule of "withdrawing only the items used," using one Kanban per component[1] is the ideal method. Despite the benefit of one Kanban per item, a single Kanban is being shared for multiple-items in many factories since purchasing and producing items in batch are usually less costly to a certain degree.

NUMBER OF DAYS AS INDICATED BY KANBANS, "DELIVERY CYCLE"

A Kanban indicates the number of days within which a component needs to be delivered after its Kanban was removed. This is called the "Delivery Cycle." It signifies a rate of transportation usually by trucks between factories and its suppliers. The following figure is an example in which a supplier delivers necessary components the day after Kanbans were received. However, in most cases, a certain number of days

---

1 In most cases, large or expensive components have a single dedicated Kanban attached to it.

are added onto delivery time after Kanbans are received for suppliers to produce necessary components to be delivered.

Reaction times of suppliers to Kanbans need to be taken into consideration in cases where the number of incoming Kanbans fluctuates depending on sales of certain products. Therefore, it is ideal that Kanbans come back to suppliers as soon as possible after they were removed from components so that suppliers can ensure delivery of components in the shortest amount of time.

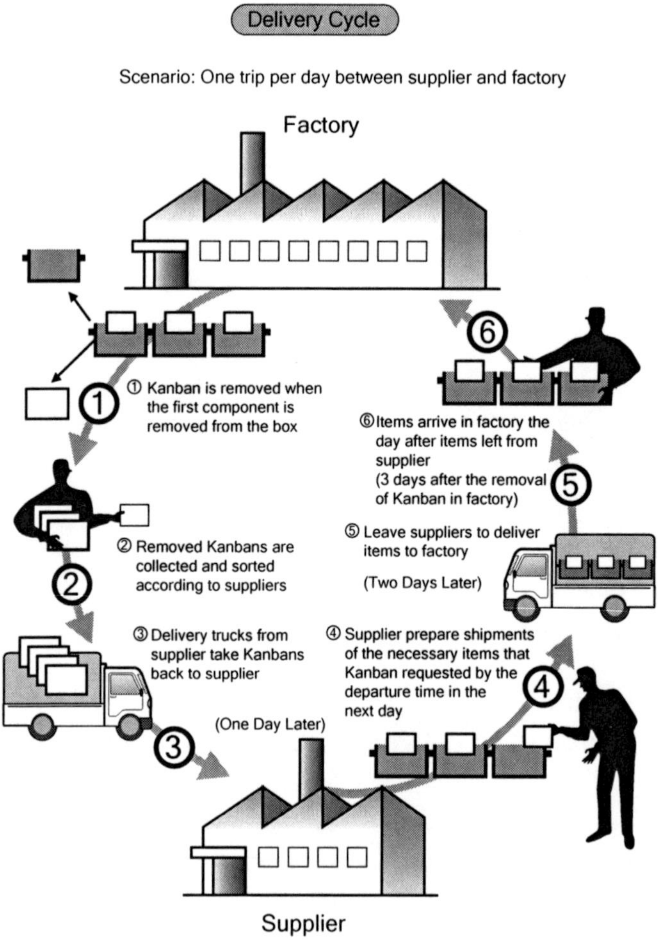

(Delivery Cycle)

Scenario: One trip per day between supplier and factory

Factory

① Kanban is removed when the first component is removed from the box

⑥ Items arrive in factory the day after items left from supplier
(3 days after the removal of Kanban in factory)

② Removed Kanbans are collected and sorted according to suppliers

⑤ Leave suppliers to deliver items to factory

(Two Days Later)

③ Delivery trucks from supplier take Kanbans back to supplier

④ Supplier prepare shipments of the necessary items that Kanban requested by the departure time in the next day

(One Day Later)

Supplier

Figure 15: Kanban Delivery Cycle

Production methods decide "Daily-use Quantity"

In addition to "Contained Quantity" and "Delivery Cycle," which provides information related to supply of components in the calculation of Kanbans, "Daily-use Quantity," describing how many components to be used daily, needs to be taken into consideration as well. "Daily-use Quantity" essentially provides information related to the demand of components.

If we produce a certain number of products every day, a quantity of the necessary component remains fixed daily. However, many factories produce multiple products daily and their finished products are usually manufactured in inconsistent quantities. Even more, different products require different components to be put together. Therefore, "Daily-use Quantity" of components varies significantly every day.

With this in mind, we allow a flexible "Daily-use Quantity" to be used in the calculation in order to avoid a shortage of components.

Production and purchasing pattern influence the number of necessary Kanbans

What would happen if we start implementing Kanbans without considering these three important factors: "Daily-use Quantity" (the quantity of components used daily), "Contained Quantity" (unit of components that needs to be ordered from suppliers) and "Delivery Cycle" (the number of days it takes for suppliers to deliver components)?

Traditionally, it is considered efficient to produce items in batch and many factories have made a habit of it. Such factories may be able to maintain a consistent rate of overall daily production, however, production time required for each product remains unpredictable from one day to the next.

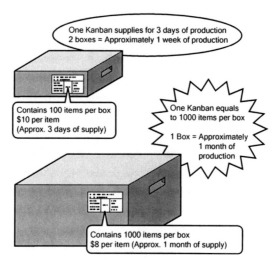

Each component costs $10 in a box of 100 units.
On the other hand, each component costs $8 in a box of 1000 units. But...

One Kanban supplies for 3 days of production
2 boxes = Approximately 1 week of production

Contains 100 items per box
$10 per item
(Approx. 3 days of supply)

One Kanban equals
to 1000 items per box

1 Box = Approximately
1 month of
production

Contains 1000 items per box
$8 per item (Approx. 1 month of supply)

*Figure 16: Number of Kanbans varies to match the needs of
Production and Purchasing patterns*

For example, if a certain product sells in a quantity of 10 per day (200 per month in other words), this product is produced in batch in a quantity of 50 on one day out of each week. However, if a product requires 3 components to be assembled together, it means that daily use of the components ranges from 0 to 50 at any given day, resulting in a great deal of irregularity in production.

In this kind of batch production, we still need to incorporate in the calculation "150" components as "Daily-use Quantity" in order to prevent shortage in components from occurring.[2] As a result, the number of Kanbans needs to be increased, leading to a large increase in inventory.

On the other hand, it is common sense in manufacturing that components are less costly if purchased in batch.[3] As a

2 For example, if the "Daily-use Quantity" is 150 for every Friday, we do not have to use 150 for the calculation. However, if it is 150 on Friday and another 150 on Monday in the following week, the value of 150 needs to be taken into consideration to be on the safe side.
3 Household items such as beer and groceries can be purchased in batch to reduce cost per item. If you buy them in bulk, they are usually less expensive.

matter of fact, suppliers often prepare their components to be shipped out in lot for their customers.

However, purchasing components in batch often leads to an excessive inventory and does not allow us to adjust the inventory according to the required production intensity at every level.[4]

Commonly used components in a given industry can be ordered from any supplier without delay. This is because suppliers usually stock these items and have them ready to be shipped out upon receiving orders.

However, suppliers may not stock components that are unique only to your company and not to others. In such a case, suppliers require a few extra days to produce the component upon receiving orders due to a shortage in stock.

The amount of time suppliers may require is also influenced by their own efficiency in production and the relation of authority that you may encounter between your factory and suppliers. As explained here, a longer delivery cycle causes the number of Kanbans to increase. The ideal scenario for Kanbans is to be removed from components on a daily basis. If they stop getting removed or remain unused for assembly due to sudden changes or a termination in production, your factory will suffer from the excess amount of inventory in addition to what you have already ordered from suppliers with previous Kanbans.

As described here, if you simply implement Kanbans without altering the conventional production[5] and purchasing methods, it is more likely that inventory will not be de-

4 If the "Contained Quantity" is 100, an inventory can be adjusted in increments of one hundred such as 100, 200, and 300. However, if it is 1,000, it can be adjusted in increments of one thousand such as 1,000, 2,000, 3,000. In the latter case, a large excess of inventory will be an adverse effect, especially when the "Daily-use Quantity" remains relatively low.
5 Many factories decide to give up on implementing Kanbans in their practices while conducting the calculation. They often calculate the number of Kanbans to be too large to manage effectively.

creased; rather, it will increase unexpectedly over a period of time.

"Contained Quantity," "Delivery Cycle" and "Daily-use Quantity" will not be automatically adjusted just because you are implementing Kanbans. They need to be carefully revised by various continuous improvement methods in conjunction with practicing Kanbans in production.

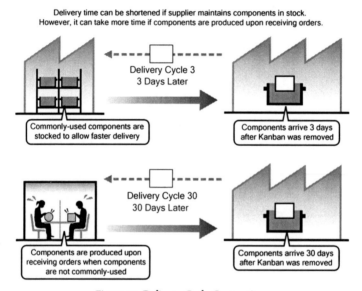

Figure 17: Delivery Cycle Comparison

Such continuous improvement efforts should focus on minimizing the number of "Contained Quantity," shortening "Delivery Cycle" and averaging daily production, in other words, removing irregularity in quantities produced daily. In fact, this very idea is what Toyota has strongly emphasized over the years in accomplishing a flow in production.

Comparison between when a daily average of 30
components are used and when 150 items are used at once.
(In a case where Delivery Cycle = 30 and Contained Quantity = 100

	Number of Kanbans	Calculation
Daily-use Quantity = 30	2	$\left(3 + 1\right) \times \dfrac{30}{100} = 1.2$
Daily-use Quantity =150	6	$\left(3 + 1\right) \times \dfrac{150}{100} = 6$

Comparison between Contained Quantity = 100 and 1000.
(In a case where Delivery Cycle = 3 and Daily-use Quantity = 30)

	Number of Kanbans	Calculation
Contained Quantity = 100	2	$\left(3 + 1\right) \times \dfrac{30}{100} = 1.2$
Contained Quantity =1,000	1	$\left(3 - 1\right) \times \dfrac{30}{1,000} = 0.12$

Even though the number of Kanbans is 1(less), the inventory
still increases due to a larger Contained Quantity.

Comparison between Delivery Cycle = 3 and 30

	Number of Kanbans	Calculation
Delivery Cycle = 3	2	$\left(3 + 1\right) \times \dfrac{30}{100} = 1.2$
Delivery Cycle = 30	10	$\left(30 + 1\right) \times \dfrac{30}{100} = 9.3$

Figure 18: Comparison Cycle Equations

In the past, producing, purchasing, and transporting in batch had become common practices in manufacturing. This is because it was considered more efficient and economically feasible to do so. However, what would happen if you implemented Kanbans without eliminating these old habits in your factory?

Most factories attempt to average the rate of production on a daily basis.[6] However, the quantities of a particular product vary significantly on a daily basis. For a product which is sold in an average of 10 units per day and of 200 units per month is usually produced in the quantity of 50 units once per week instead of 10 units per day.

In such case, the "Daily-use Quantity" of 150 components is required, given that a product utilizes 3 components to be assembled together. This is obviously more than 30 components required for producing 10 units per day as recommended and as a result, leads to irregularity in daily production output.

The key to achieving a flow in production is to ensure minimized lot sizes for components (smaller "Contained Quantity"), frequent deliveries of components (shortening "Delivery Cycle") and averaging daily production output (averaging "Daily-use Quantity").

However, it is extremely hard to create a consistent flow in production like the steady flow of water in a well-maintained canal. Production may experience "waves" within itself to a certain degree. Our efforts need to focus on turning those waves into never-ending gentle ripples, so to speak.

It would be extremely disastrous if a quiet river suddenly flooded and its levees were destroyed. However, if the water level of a river increased gradually by ripples, we could pre-

---

6 This is to control and minimize the labor cost of their employees, which is heavily influenced by the daily production volume.

vent such a flood by sandbagging banks of the river well in advance.

The same analogy can be applied to production as far as the Toyota System is concerned. If a tidal wave suddenly hit a factory, the shop floors would be in a great panic like working bees would in their attached hive. The ideal is to average daily work so that production output should increase or decrease in small increments. By doing that, you will be able to successfully manage both your own limited inventory and limited supplies from your vendors.

However, it will take a great deal of time for the shop floor that prioritizes batch production for maximizing production efficiency to incorporate a one-piece flow.

It is not easy to ask suppliers to maintain the same price for a smaller batch of components. For example, item prices cannot be maintained if a supplier is demanded to arrange 100 units per batch instead of 1000 units per batch and to shorten their delivery time to 3 days from 30 days. Such requests often require long-term negotiations[7] with suppliers, or are simply rejected by them.

As I've described, the Kanban System is not effective if it is adopted only as a tool for transferring data. It becomes truly effective only after a flow in production is achieved on the shop floor. In other words, the Kanban System may not yield any desired results depending on how you decide to carry it out. Moreover, it can also lead to cost increase within your own company and suppliers. Let me illustrate with some examples in the next section.

---

7 In some cases, negotiations can continue on for a few months to a year.

3-3 Kanbans Can Become Deadly Weapons If Not Used Properly

On February 3rd, 1978, the state of the Kanban System in Japanese industry was mentioned in the House of Representatives as follows:

"Sub-contractors or suppliers receive actual orders by phone the day before items need to be shipped out. For example, orders are received at 3:00 p.m. and are expected to be delivered by 10:00 a.m. the next morning. In some cases, orders need to be delivered three or four times a day on a regular basis like: 10:00 a.m., 3:00 p.m., 10:00 p.m., and 3:00 a.m., or 9:30 a.m., 11:30 a.m., and 1:30 p.m., depending on the rate of production. What is worse is that purchase orders do not tell us how many orders are coming in for a given day. Sometimes, we need to stay up all night to prepare shipments, or do absolutely nothing without any orders coming in. Due to this inconsistency in order placing, Kanbans have significantly changed the way in which business is conducted between factories and suppliers. As far as I know, a number of business owners are stressed out and are complaining about Kanbans."

Is something like this really happening?

KANBAN'S FORECAST IS NOT USUALLY CORRECT

Component suppliers and sub-contractors receive, on a daily basis, Kanbans once to a several times a day.[8] Suppliers prepare components in the quantity specified by a Kanban (multiply that amount by the number of Kanbans if more than one Kanban is received) and deliver items at a specific "Delivery Cycle" indicated by the Kanban.

---

8 Factories outside the Toyota Group rarely receive Kanbans at multiple times in the same day.

A big problem here is that the number of Kanbans cannot be predicted beforehand. To avoid confusion among suppliers, factories provide their suppliers in advance with a forecast as to how many Kanbans will be sent out. However, it is only an unofficial announcement and is not guaranteed to be always accurate. In this case, factories often make an excuse for their forecast being inaccurate. They may claim that the number of Kanbans that suppliers are responsible for is unpredictable because it is heavily dependant on the volume of their sales on a daily basis.

In fact, the sales volume is not the only factor to explain inconsistency in how many Kanbans are handed out to suppliers. There are many other factors in factories that lead to this inconsistency.

BATCH PROCESSING REGENERATES THE WAVES OF INCONSISTENCY

Companies that have not adopted the Toyota System generally perform batch-processing on the shop floors as well as in other administrative duties. For example, it is troublesome to keep ordering the same component everyday. Ordering components in batch saves time by submitting only a few purchase orders instead of multiple purchase orders a day. It also allows us to have to perform inspection much less frequently than we would if we ordered components on a daily basis.

However, if such batch processing was carried out under the Kanban System, suppliers may face a great risk of having to supply more items than usual if the factory unexpectedly experiences a dramatic increase in sales of certain products for a given day.

Suppliers expect Kanbans to come in at a consistent rate. If the number of Kanbans fluctuates every day or requires much more quantity than usual, the Kanban System becomes a deadly weapon against suppliers just like it did in the story of the supplier in the Japanese Parliament meeting. In the next section, I will explain the adverse effects Kanbans.

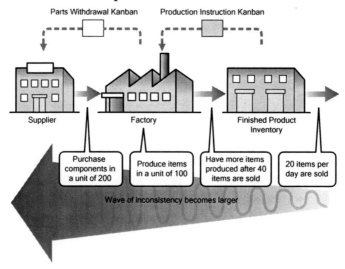

Figure 19: Production Waves of Inconsistency

ADVERSE EFFECT OF KANBANS #1
"KANBANS INCREASE INVENTORY"

In an extreme case where a significantly large number of Kanbans were given to suppliers, workers may have to work overtime to arrange the shipments to be delivered by the deadlines. To avoid working overtime, workers start producing components in batch, especially on slow days so that they will be ready to supply items for busier days. However, this will naturally increase their inventories.

This would not be an issue at all if they continued to receive order Kanbans in a constant manner and their inventories were consumed over time as a result. However, this is not always true in practice. Many products these days have a short life cycle[9], which may cause Kanbans not to be as consistently ordered on a daily basis. Consequently, suppliers would have to eliminate excess inventories. This is a chal-

9 As new products are continually developed, sold and supplied to customers, marketability of a single product has significantly shortened.

lenge because the supplier has to pay for the costs associated with removing such inventories rather than consuming them over time.

ADVERSE EFFECT OF KANBANS #2
"KANBANS INCREASE THE NUMBER OF NECESSARY WORKERS"

Kanbans certainly change the way suppliers operate from accepting orders to shipping orders. In the past, batches of orders would come in by mail, or electronically, well in advance so that suppliers had enough time to confirm and prepare the necessary items by deadlines.

However, under the Kanban System, Kanbans are received every day and components must be immediately put into designated boxes with new Kanbans attached before they are delivered by trucks by certain deadlines. This means that various changes need to be accommodated in the processes of transferring data and delivering items and even how orders are written.

Especially in the early stage of adopting Kanbans, factories often practice a new Kanban method in addition to their traditional ways in order to administrate their production and logistic operations, which often leads to an increase in labor time and cost. Consequently, the number of workers that are needed will increase as well.

ADVERSE EFFECT OF KANBANS #3
"KANBANS INCREASE THE COST OF TRANSPORTATION"

If Kanbans are not implemented, factories rarely need to supply components every day. Rather, in most cases, components are delivered once in a few business days. This is because delivering components every day is costly, which will eventually be reflected in the price of such components. In other words, it is advantageous for factories to order components in batch as infrequently as possible. In addition, if a supplier is able to transport a supply of components for two days in one track, they would rather choose to transport everything in one day.

However, under the Kanban System, suppliers are requested to deliver components on a daily basis instead of delivering them say, every other day, as in the past. In such a case, the daily truck load is obviously close to zero.

In the past, some suppliers were able to ship all the necessary components in a single box by air. If they are asked to ship only the necessary components by the same method every day, it would be extremely costly for them no matter what. Usually, the cost of transportation is prepaid by suppliers, or rather transportation cost is already included in the price of their items. However, suppliers are often compelled to absorb this cost[10] to maintain the prices of their items in order to avoid losing their customers.

---

10 Suppliers simply start rejecting the request from factories to deliver components on a daily basis and continue to deliver items irregularly in spite of Kanbans.

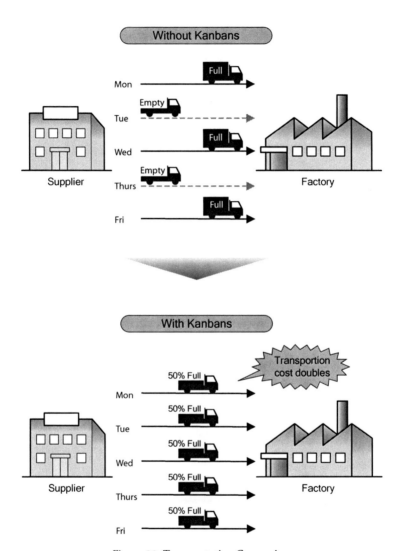

Figure 20: Transportation Comparison

Kanbans require factories to change the manner of their operations as well. For example, if a supplier delivers components using their own drivers, it is easy to ask the driver to take back the Kanbans to his own factory. On the other hand, if a supplier uses a third party delivery company or ships a package, it is extremely hard to have Kanbans returned to the supplier. In such case, factories must figure out an effective way to return Kanbans[11] to their suppliers.

Kanbans are basically made of paper so mailing them is, of course, possible. However, the mailing method involves putting Kanbans in envelopes, printing addresses, putting stamps on and taking envelopes to a post office. These tasks need to be repeatedly carried out everyday, which eventually leads to an increase in administrative costs.

As I mentioned before, suppliers are forced to bear the increased costs of labor and delivering items. But, some suppliers may balance the costs by demanding to sell their items at higher prices. The purchasing department of a factory would do its best not to accept such a demand from suppliers, which makes it more difficult for the factory to negotiate for lower prices from suppliers in the future. Suppliers would also become reluctant to be responsible for any Kanbans that indicate quantities quite different from what had been forecasted.

In this case, it is expected that the shop floor would be booed by different departments such as purchasing and sales even though the shop floor was successful in reducing the size of inventory. Other departments in the factory were forced to bear this adverse effect of Kanbans. The size of inventory may have been decreased, but the cost associated with achieving that increased the overall cost of production. As a result, Kanbans could become a deadly weapon not only

---

11 Sending back Kanbans by fax is possible but is not usually a practical method of transporting in practice.

against suppliers but also against your own factory.

Going back to the Japanese Parliament story at the beginning of this chapter, the factory in question may have started using Kanbans before they had successfully achieved a flow in production. This kind of incident is often apparent in factories that mimic the Toyota System without understanding its core principles. In this chapter I have illustrated some examples of the adverse effects of Kanbans. We need to remember that there are still some factories that treat suppliers unfairly with the wrong uses of Kanbans.

4. Cell Production and Kanbans Become Misfortune Without Overall Optimization

4-1 The Time When Positive Results of Cell Production Vanish

Is "Cell Production" a part of the Toyota System?

Many people associate "Cell Production" with the Toyota System next to Kanbans. Cell Production is a production system that has been widely practiced on the shop floors in electronics and machinery manufactures.

The famous books written about the Toyota System do not write about Cell Production. However, since it incorporates many principles associated with the Toyota System, it is considered as an important part of the Toyota System in some cases.

Cell Production takes many different forms. It is basically a method in which small groups of workers are put together to complete a product from beginning to end. The most important method is called "One Person Work Cell Production," in which a designated worker performs a series of processes on his own[1] in a designated area. In contrary to this One-Person Work Cell, there is a traditional method, "Line Production on a Conveyor Belt," in which multiple workers are assigned to complete production in a line.

The Cell Production System is capable of bringing out positive results in production but it can still fail to yield positive results in some cases. In this chapter, I will talk about the challenges of the Toyota System from the perspective of Cell Production.

INFLEXIBLE CONVEYOR BELT PRODUCTION VS VERSATILE CELL PRODUCTION

Production performed on a conveyor belt cannot be sped up any more than the maximum speed at which it can move. For example, when 100 products can be manufactured at the maximum speed, no more than 100 products can be manufactured no matter how hard workers may try. On the other hand, if a worker delays his operation in the production line, production can decrease as low as 50%.

Additional lines of conveyor belts need to be put into the shop floor to accommodate expansion of production as sales increase. This requires a significant amount of money to invest into new equipment. It is disastrous if product sales go down in the middle of installing new conveyor belts.

Production is expected to increase in an increment of 100 units for every new conveyor belt that is adopted. If the factory demands to increase product from 100 units to 120 units by adding a new conveyor belt, it would be an overabundance of capital. This illustrates the inflexibility found in line

---

1 Multiple workers can be assigned to a single work cell as well.

production. How can the One-Person Cell Production System solve this problem?

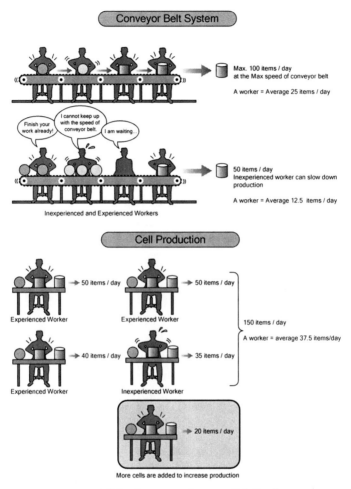

Figure 21: Cell Production vs. Conveyor Belt Production

In the case of Cell Production, production can be increased in much smaller increments by adding additional work cells[2]. It is a much less risky way to increase production as it does not require an extensive investment of capital such as conveyor belts would.

In addition, an expert worker is able to boost his performance significantly in a work cell environment instead

2 Work cells can be easily constructed by using plastic pipes and joints. They are much easier to install than conveyor belts on the shop floor.

of being limited by the speed of a conveyor belt. Such an expert worker will be able to do as much work as two workers combined would do on a conveyor belt. In some cases, it is common to observe 10 workers in work cells to produce as much as 150 units instead of 100 units that was originally the maximum output on conveyor belts.

BATCH PROCESSING INCREASES INVENTORY OF PROCESSED COMPONENTS

Cell Production is also effective for performing divided work in batch processing.

Let me explain the basics of an assembly process. When a certain product is manufactured it is divided into large sections first, and then each section is assembled individually. This is called "sub-assembly" or "unit assembly." Assembled sections are put together to become a finished product at the final stage of production. This final stage of assembly is called "main assembly" or "total assembly."

For a bicycle, it is divided into sections such as the frame, front wheel, rear wheel, and handlebars. Each section is assembled together at the final stage to become a complete bicycle.

What needs to be done differently if more than one kind of bicycle, such as a sport bicycle, kid bicycle, and an all-purpose bicycle are to be manufactured?

Traditionally, it was thought to be more efficient to produce one kind at a time. If each kind needs to be manufactured in the quantity of 100 units, each section for a particular kind is sub-assembled independently from other kinds. After sub-assembly, sections are put together at last. It would look something like this: produce 100 units of sport bicycles, then 100 units of kid bicycles, and 100 units of all-purpose bicycles. Finally, quality inspection is carried out for each kind in the quantity of 100.

As a matter of fact, bicycle frames require a number of components and take more time to produce than to manufacture handlebars. Wheels also require more time to be delivered to the shop floor if they are manufactured by suppliers. In this case, no matter how soon the handlebars are ready, the assembly line has no choice but to wait until frames and wheels arrive at the shop floor to be assembled. This waiting period causes processed components to be held on the shop floor.

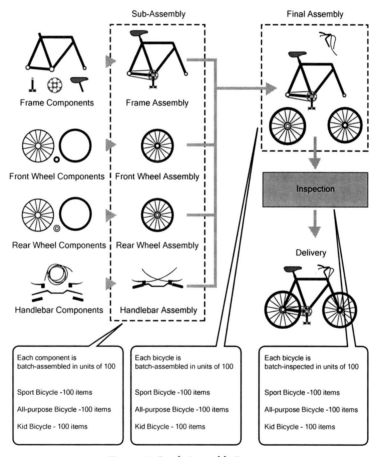

Figure 22: Batch Assembly Process

Such inventory of processed components[3] causes an adverse impact on production in the same manner as inventories of finished products and unprocessed components would.

HOW WOULD CELL PRODUCTION DEAL WITH THE SAME SITUATION?

A single worker is responsible for performing the entire assembling process of a bicycle in our case of Cell Production. That worker assembles the bike from handlebars to wheels, as well as the final assembly, to deliver a complete bicycle.

Therefore, Cell Production reduces inventories of processed sections on the shop floor of your factory, since processed sections can be utilized immediately in the following process. In the past, inspection was carried out after the 100th bicycle is completed which resulted in longer production time per product. However, Cell Production carries out inspection upon completion of each product, through which production time per item can be reduced significantly.

As described, Cell Production is a very flexible and attractive system because it is able to adjust its production output, depending on supply and demand, while maximizing skills of workers and reducing the overall production cost. Inventory of finished products can also be drastically reduced as Cell Production allows factories to produce only the products in the quantity that they are sold.

---

3 Already processed components that reside either between processes or within a process.

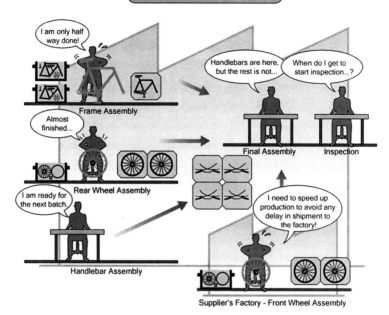

Figure 23: Batch Production Factory Process

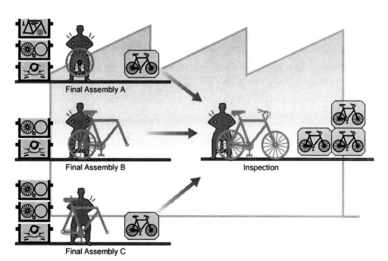

Figure 24: Cell Production Factory Process

Efficient delivery of the necessary components to work cells is the key to a successful application of Cell Production. In line production, workers need to place the necessary components near a conveyor belt at the beginning of every workday. On the other hand, in Cell Production, each worker has to retrieve only the necessary components to be used in the required quantity from a warehouse every morning. It is troublesome to make frequent trips to a warehouse every time components run out from work cells. Instead, a worker chooses to withdraw components in batch to avoid more trips, which often causes their work cells to be cluttered with unprocessed components.

If a worker is responsible for assembling only a certain product over and over, this method may be manageable. However, if a worker assembles many different kinds of products in the same day he will face a difficult challenge of retrieving all the necessary components in a timely manner.

To overcome this problem, the Toyota System assigns certain workers to deliver components to work cells so that work cell workers do not need to retrieve the items on their own. Such designated workers are called "Water Spiders,"[4] moving like a water spider between work cells and component storage rooms to deliver necessary items to work cell workers.

If a "Water Spider" delivers components then cell workers no longer need to hunt for components by themselves and are able to focus on their assembly task for the entire day. Cell workers are also able to organize and maximize space in their work cell environment as they no longer need to deal with a clutter of unprocessed components.

---

4 Insects that are usually found hovering on the surfaces of a lake or pond. It is about 7mm in length.

Assigning certain workers as "Water Spiders," though, may pose a risk of having to manage extra manpower. However, the total number of workers in the factory rarely increases as the workers in work cells become more capable to boost their productivity over time.

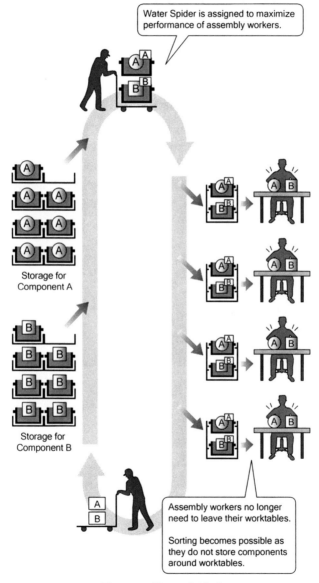

Figure 25: "Water Spider"

Daily average use of components can be successfully achieved by a flow that is created by "Water Spiders" transporting only the necessary items between assembly lines and inventories. On the other hand, if components are processed more than necessary in a preceding process, or were purchased in batch, factories will experience an excess amount of components if "Water Spiders" transport only the essential items in the necessary quantity. It is often expected that factories can achieve non-stock production by reducing the amount of processed inventory by using the Cell Production method. However, it is not as easy as we can expect because the unprocessed components that are leftover on the shop floor also need to be eliminated to achieve a true non-stock production.

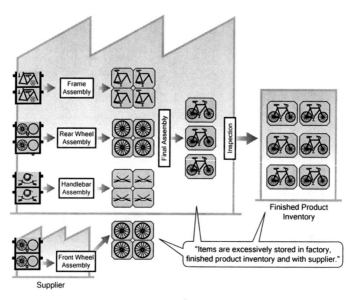

Figure 26: Unprocessed Component Inventory

Inventories in a factory can be divided in 3 types, "Finished Product Inventory," "Processed Component Inventory," and "Unprocessed Component Inventory (Raw Material Inventory)." Adopting Cell Production designed to generate only the right product types in the right quantity can drastically reduce both "Finished Products Inventory" and "Processed Component Inventory." However, this method alone does not reduce the amount of "Unprocessed Component Inventory."

HOW TO REDUCE "UNPROCESSED COMPONENT INVENTORY"

What can be done to reduce the amount of "Unprocessed Component Inventory"?

The example of Cell Production for the bicycle assembly demonstrated a case where continuous improvement effort was focused only on the final stage of production to achieve one-piece flow. To expand the benefit of one-piece flow over the entire production, earlier stages of production must also be continuously improved.

For example, if an assembly process follows a preceding process, only the necessary components that are needed for assembly should be produced in the right quantity by the preceding process.

To accommodate this, machinery needs to be optimized to produce different types of components on a daily basis. In the past, machinery would have to produce only a few kinds of items but modern machinery is designed for producing many kinds of items. Workers have to set up machinery with the right tools, such as blades and clasps, more frequently according to the component to be manufactured. These setup times increase the overall production time.

If machinery needs to be setup twice a day, it only requires a total of two hours to complete, given that it takes one hour to complete a single setup. However, if setups are required four times a day, workers need to spend a total of four hours on rearranging machinery. As a result, workers end up having much less actual production time available[5] to produce the necessary components at bare minimum. Therefore, setup time needs to be shortened as much as possible.

Production under the Toyota System requires workers to set up machinery multiple times a day to maintain one-piece production. Therefore, continuous improvement ideas should begin to be implemented on the shop floor to shorten setup time as much as possible.

As a matter of fact, many factories have succeeded in reducing setup times to less than 10 minutes.[6] This is a good example of how a desire to achieve a certain goal can generate consistent continuous improvement efforts on the shop floor.

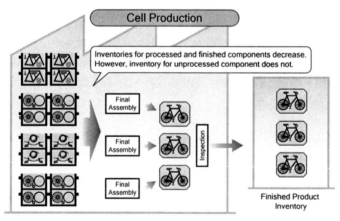

Figure 27: Cell Production Reduces Unprocessed Component Inventory

All preceding processes need to initiate continuous improvement efforts so that the positive effects of Cell Production can be spread to the rest of the production line. To achieve that, post-processes must also perform a certain continuous improvement method, as follows.

For example, a factory produces a total 500 units per week. Perhaps it produces 300 units of product A and 200 units of Product B per week. In the past, it was considered more efficient to batch produce each item separately. The factory would produce 300 units of product A from Monday through Wednesday and 200 units of product B from Thursday through Friday.

To achieve success with this method, the necessary components for 300 units need to be delivered on Monday morning, as well as those for 200 units that need to be delivered on Thursday morning, to the shop floor.

What happens if this production method is changed to Cell Production, in which both the components for 60 units of product A and 40 units of product B are delivered every morning to work cells?

This would allow preceding processes to prepare consistent amounts of components to be assembled on a daily basis with the same amount of labor. In addition, storages would only require enough space to accommodate components for 100 units per day. These positive outcomes will stabilize production to a great degree.

As I have illustrated above, it is important to establish a production system designed to optimize efficiency in every part of production. This can be achieved by consistent continuous improvement efforts that focus not only in work cell environments but also in relationships between preceding and post-processes.

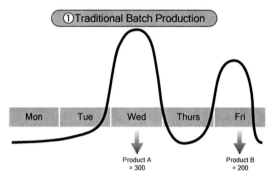

Figure 28: Traditional Batch Production Operation

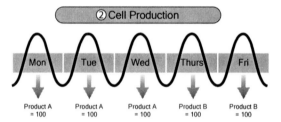

Figure 29: Cell Production Operation

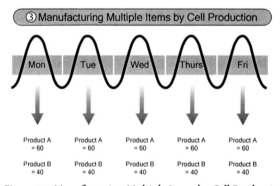

Figure 30: Manufacturing Multiple Items by Cell Production

4-2 Spreading Improvements from Factories to Suppliers

Inventory reduction cannot be achieved only by a partial improvement on the shop floor, such as adopting a Cell Production method. The way in which raw materials and components are purchased from suppliers needs to be revised in order to achieve inventory reduction. From the stand point of factories, it is ideal to purchase only the necessary components at the right time. However, this should not be forced upon suppliers or your factory may experience adverse effects.

The first priority for factories is to equalize the usage of raw materials and components. After that is accomplished, factories must shift away from purchasing components in batch only for the purpose of acquiring lower prices from suppliers. Then the factory can establish a secure traffic system so that Parts Withdrawal Kanbans can be delivered smoothly between production and suppliers.

THE WALL OF PURCHASING ITEMS IN BATCH MAINLY FOR KEEPING THE PRICES LOW

Buyers of components have a strong desire to buy them in batch as much as the sellers wish to sell components in batch. Especially for buyers, if more components are purchased at the same time, the price per component becomes significantly lower than when purchased by itself. Production companies will never allow the slightest increase in the cost of components no matter how desperately they need to achieve a better production flow. This is the biggest wall-of-resistance that exists here.

Additionally, in the process of ordering components, purchase orders must inform suppliers of "What" components needed to be delivered by "When" and "How many." Ordering 20 components per day will be required to maintain a flow and ordering a batch of 100 components once a week will never achieve such a flow in production. Placing orders on a regular basis also increase administrative costs. In this case, it will be increased by 5 times because 5 orders are placed to order 20 items separately instead of placing a single order to order 100 items at once.

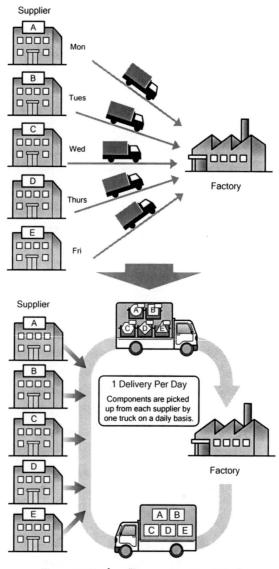

Figure 31: Kanban "Procurement Logistics"

It would not do factories any good unless ordered components arrive at the shop floor from suppliers on time. However, if the purchasing department is already experiencing delivery delays from suppliers, it would be close to impossible to demand more frequent deliveries. This is the main reason why factories choose not to impose any changes over suppliers.

THE WALL OF PARTS WITHDRAWAL KANBANS

Parts Withdrawal Kanbans are used to order components from suppliers in the Toyota System. There are many problems associated with utilizing Kanbans as purchase orders.

As I mentioned before, the fact that Kanbans are made of paper and need to be physically transported to suppliers is the main cause of problems. Kanbans can be easily returned if suppliers use their own trucks and drivers to deliver components, but in some cases, Kanbans need to be sent by mail or by small parcel services back to suppliers. In addition, suppliers can suffer from this increased cost of delivery and labor so much that they no longer find any benefit in practicing Kanbans.

"PROCUREMENT LOGISTICS" CAN SOLVE THE PROBLEM OF KANBAN TRAFFIC

Parts Withdrawal Kanbans seem to be quite problematic. However, the installation of "Procurement Logistics" can solve problems associated with getting Kanbans back to suppliers in a timely manner.

Traditionally, suppliers would deliver components using their own trucks or hiring delivery companies. What would happen if we changed that and made factories (buyers) pick up components directly from their suppliers? For example, in the past daily delivery of components was alternated by suppliers such as Monday by Supplier A, Tuesday by Supplier

B, Wednesday by Supplier C, Thursday by Suppler D and Friday by Supplier E. Instead of doing it this way, a factory sends out its own truck to pick up components from Suppliers A-E and returns back on a daily basis. This guarantees that all the necessary components will arrive on the shop floor without increasing the number of trucks.

With this method, the transportation cost imposed on factories can be an issue. In most cases, it is often absorbed by suppliers, but it can be used as a tool for factories to demand suppliers to reduce the price of components. Pickup service of a factory successfully solves the issue with Parts Withdrawal Kanbans that fail to be transported back to suppliers. All a factory has to do is to load used Kanbans onto their pickup trucks and drop them off at each supplier, A-E, while new orders of components are picked up at the same time.

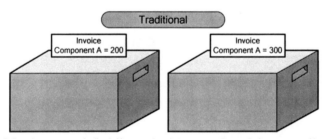

Delivery boxes are standardized. However, they do not necessarily contain the same quantities.

Figure 32: Traditional Supplier Packaging

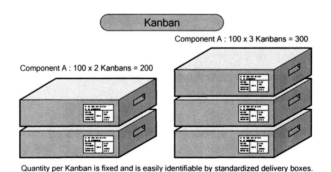

Quantity per Kanban is fixed and is easily identifiable by standardized delivery boxes.

Figure 33: Supplier Packaging Simplified with Kanbans

Traditionally, suppliers needed to be very careful to make sure that the right components in the right quantities were shipped out from their facilities. There was no clear indications as to when the components actually had to be delivered to the factories. Shipping managers would have to go through a pile of purchase orders just to find the right information. However, Parts Withdrawal Kanbans allow suppliers to prepare orders in advance. Each package contains the same number of components inside. All they have to do is attach Kanbans to an appropriate number of packages and ship them out the next day.

Parts Withdrawal Kanbans also increase the total number of Kanbans that are received by suppliers on a daily basis. However, an advantage is that each Kanban clearly tells "What" components need to be transported in "How Many" and by "When." This makes it much easier for suppliers to prepare shipments, making other operations such as packaging and administrative work much simpler for them to perform.

Factories are the ultimate hosts of a Kanban System and should play an important role in explaining to their suppliers how daily work becomes more efficient and will become more simplified by incorporating Kanbans. Without such explanations, it would be impossible to ask suppliers for their cooperation to make Kanban Systems work successfully.

With procurement logistics in place, suppliers may feel that it is possible to accommodate Kanbans. However, suppliers will be required to revise their overall workflow including how shipments are prepared. Potential increases in the cost associated with accommodating new changes also needs to be absorbed by suppliers in some cases.

As you can tell, working with Kanbans is far from being simple. However, the Kanban System is able to bring a sharp competitive edge if implemented with a high level of assurance. For example, suppliers may become capable of stealing a competitor's business if components can be delivered much more efficiently to their clients with the use of Kanbans.

Do not force suppliers. Ask for their assistance in practicing Kanbans

A thorough explanation of Kanbans must be given to any supplier when Parts Withdrawal Kanbans are to be used between your factory and theirs. Suppliers should also be invited to visit your shop floor to have the various advantages of Kanbans on the overall process explained.

If a supplier provides processing of components, they can be invited to your own component processing shop floor to be shown how Kanbans from the following assembly processes can be transmitted, and affect the ways in which components are being processed. It is also important to visit your supplier's shop floor frequently. By doing so, you will be able to provide suppliers with direct instructions pertaining to how Kanbans should be understood and handled, especially in a shipping department.

The Toyota System is based on the coexistence and mutual prosperity with suppliers

Positive results from practicing consistent continuous improvement efforts are not limited to only reducing inventory in your own factory. Such positive results can also be expanded to achieve improvement in suppliers. By reducing production lead time through eliminating the supplier's inventory of finished product, as well as processed and unprocessed components, suppliers will be able to experience an increase in sales and the betterment of their companies.

Often we hear people use the expression, "win-win situation." In most cases, people misuse this phrase for their own benefit or for cases in which it is not necessarily applicable. However, the relationship between Toyota and their suppliers is a true example of what can be described as a "win-win situation."

4-3 Results of Continuous Improvement in Factories are Not Reflected in Sales Department

SALES PEOPLE CONSISTENTLY DEMAND FACTORIES TO STOCK INVENTORY

Even though an excess amount of inventory should be eliminated by continuous improvements, and products should also be manufactured as needed based on sales demand, factories are still suffering from their inability to reduce the actual inventory. Why is that?

The ability to reduce inventory is a big advantage for business management. On the other hand, maintaining inventory at all times poses a great risk to management. However, it would become a real risk if products did not get sold and remained as leftover inventory. For this reason, sales people view inventory quite differently from the rest of us.

Production teams and sales teams meet regularly to hold discussions in which a sales projection is finalized and the amount of inventory to be held is carefully determined to accommodate sales. In this case, each sales person calculates his own sales forecast and the sales department submits the total sales projection, with room to spare, to stay on the safe side. Production is then asked to produce inventory based on this sales projection, which in fact may have predicted more than what is really needed.

From a different perspective, sales people cannot sell unless actual sales items already exist. Having inventory gives sales people the assurance of being able to supply their customers with products as soon as orders are received. In short, they would prefer having an extra amount of inventory, rather than have to deal with a shortage of products.

REALITY ASSOCIATED WITH INVENTORY OF THE FINISHED PRODUCTS

Given that maintaining absolutely zero inventories may be impossible to achieve, having only a small amount in inventories after sales is more realistic for factories, but still remains as a challenge.

If the same number of items is leftover in inventories as that of sold items, sales profit will be sacrificed. In some cases, you will find dust covered boxes that have been stored as unsold items in warehouse storage for many months, even years.

Factories cannot be held responsible for excess inventories as they follow instructions from their sales department. Sales departments cannot be blamed either as forecasts of this nature are usually inaccurate in business.

The problem is that shortages result from maintaining a low volume of inventories. This influences not only the loss of sales, but also the work performance of every sales person — no matter how hard the inventory maintenance department tries to reduce inventories. In fact, it is most difficult to maintain a bare minimum of inventories while avoiding shortages of products to be sold. In practice, most factories choose to maintain an excess of inventory and dispose of any unsold items that are left in stock. Costs associated with eliminating such stock are already included in the budget in some companies.

Sales representatives do not trust factories

Factories try to make many suggestions for not holding excess inventories. They try to convince the sales department that products can be prepared diligently as orders arrive and inventories can be restocked in a timely manner.

However, sales representatives know better than to trust factories, especially those who have had a bad experience with not being able to provide their customers with products on time. Sales reps demand factories to hold an excess amount of inventories that are set by their sales projections. The more experienced a sales representative is, the less likely he trusts factories in this respect.

What kinds of interactions were commonly practiced between sales representatives and factories? Every sales representative has his or her share of bad experiences of not being able to provide products to their customers due to a shortage of inventories. Sales representatives can place an order to factories if there are no inventories, but factories may sometimes require as long as two months until the product is ready to be delivered to the customer. Sales representatives would have to negotiate with factories for production time as their customers are less likely to wait for two months and may cancel the order. Even if sales people and factories agreed on a certain deadline by which a product is produced, the representatives would still not trust factories because of the failures from the past.

Excuses from factories

Factories present a good argument as well. Orders from sales people are not to be taken seriously, and quick delivery of certain products would bring chaos to the shop floor if such requests were granted to sales people. In some cases, factories require two months for production to be on the safe side, as instructions from sales people are very vague. This is a typical interaction between factories and sales people.

Even if sales people were told that production time was significantly reduced to one week from two months because of various continuous improvement methods in place, they would still not believe the factories, and demand inventories to be maintained excessively.

On the other hand, factories would decide not to inform sales people of their shortened production time in some cases. This is to accommodate cases in which factories may fail to meet deadlines or sales people force unreasonable requests. In such a case, factories may ask sales people for a month and a half, to complete production without disclosing the fact that it can actually be done within a week.

This type of relationship between factories and sales people is the main reason why factories cannot pull themselves out of production planning in which products need to be pre-made based on sales projection.

FACTORIES MAINTAIN THE RESPONSIBILITY FOR CONTROLLING INVENTORIES

Shortened production time as a result of small-lot production and a flow method allows factories to manufacture products according to sales and significantly reduce the amount of inventories to be maintained. However, if factories strive to leave behind their old way of planning, they need to remove themselves from the allowance in production time, and refrain from preparing the excess amount of inventories so sales people can simply make more sales. This is the biggest challenge in managing inventories for finished products.

To overcome this challenge, factories need to take the initiative and attempt to establish new relationships with sales people. Even though the problem may arise from inaccurate sales projections, the need to accommodate unsold stocks at the end will bring fatal damage to the company on a larger scale; the shop floor in particular. Given this factor, factories should declare that they are totally responsible for controlling inventories for finished products.

Factories continue to implement many other continuous improvement efforts even after having achieved the ability to produce items according to sales volume within a shortened production time allowed. For these continuous improvement methods to carry on and a low volume of inventories to be maintained, full control over how inventories are managed should be put into the hands of factories, not sales people.

COMMUNICATION BETWEEN SALES REPRESENTATIVES AND FACTORIES IS IMPORTANT

It is also important to keep factories informed of sales trends for the purpose of reducing product inventories. In particular, information regarding sales trends should not be biased by the convenience of sales people.

For example, there are many cases in which the number of actual sales orders increases towards the end of each month. There seem to be many reasons other than customers simply deciding to place orders toward the end of each month.

In fact, most sales representatives are managed with sales quotas. Their performance is reviewed in terms of their likelihood of achieving their annual sales quota on a yearly basis. In some cases, such reviews take place on a monthly basis. In this case, some sales representatives may decide to work hard only toward the end of a month. A low volume of inventories should be sufficient if sales people choose to average their sales every day. If sales are concentrated on the end of a month, the volume of inventories to be maintained has the potential to grow.

Given that, there is a limit to how much production can be improved if sales people do not change their ways. This is true regardless of how hard factories attempt to reduce inventories by their continuous improvement methods.

Sales representatives must make every effort within their own department to find an effective way of informing factories of sales trends without altering information. On the other hand, factories must also disclose to sales people any improvements made to production, and eliminate the negative image of factories that sales representatives may have encountered in the past. Effective communication methods need to be established in order to build this kind of new relationship between factories and sales departments.

5. ABSENCE OF PARTICIPATION FROM TOP MANAGEMENT LEADS TO WAR WITHOUT CODES

5-1 War Without Codes Between Departments

IS THERE A WAR WITHOUT CODES BETWEEN DEPARTMENTS?

"War without Codes"[1] may be a bit of an exaggeration, but conflicts between different departments do occur when the Toyota System comes into practice. These conflicts do not involve any physical hitting or shooting, of course. In most cases, departments experience arguments and an awkward atmosphere develops against other departments.

This is because the Toyota System begins to promote the full optimization of an entire company by integrating continuous improvement. In the past, it focused only on a partial

---

1 A phrase "War without Codes" was popularized by the movie titled "War without Codes", which was based on a true story of gangs in the post-war Hiroshima city.

optimization of selected departments. In other words, not only factories, but also departments such as sales, purchasing, and other departments that have an indirect relationship with factories, need to change the way work is performed to improve production.

These conflicts, as a result of implementation of the Toyota System, should be seen as being for the betterment of the company. The Toyota System brings various unseen problems to the surface within departments that were only partially optimized in the past. Overcoming such conflicts allows the Toyota System to step forward in achieving the full optimization of a company. Unfortunately, many companies fail to overcome this challenge in reality. I will explain why the implementation of the Toyota System causes conflicts among departments with some examples.

Processing Department vs. Assembly Department
"Pick up the components right away!"

In the past, preceding processes would send all processed components on to the following post-processes. However, post-processes retrieve only the required components from preceding processes when needed under the Toyota System. In such a case, preceding processes should not make more components than what the Kanbans indicate, otherwise they would suffer an excess amount of components. The same problem can occur if post-processes practice batch processing of components only to boost the efficiency of production.

In the example of the bicycle factory, before the Toyota System was introduced different types of bicycles such as sport bicycles, kids bicycles, and all-purpose bicycles were assembled in batches of 100 on a weekly basis. However, the Toyota System introduced a way to assemble a daily average of five bicycles per kind on a daily basis, which required post-process to retrieve only the necessary amount of frames for five bicycles per day.

On the other hand, the preceding processes that continued to batch process the amount of frames required for 100 bicycles began to suffer from a shortage of space to store the remaining components after a daily required amount of only five bicycles is retrieved by post-process.

Workers in preceding processes do not have any idea about the benefits of the Toyota System since it was initiated on the shop floor of post processes. They would not know what to do with the remaining components if post-processes refused to retrieve them all of a sudden. Some workers in preceding processes often go as far as bringing all the remaining components to post-processes to be accepted.

INSPECTION DEPARTMENT VS. PRODUCTION DEPARTMENT
"INSPECTION CANNOT BE DONE HERE"

Inspection and production departments are located in different areas in most factories. The inspection department is responsible for examining the quality of finished products that are delivered by the production department. Finished products need to be transported in batch to the inspection department since it is usually located far from production. In some cases, finished products are collected and transported only once a day. However, transporting finished products only once a day poses some serious problems. If defects are present among the finished products to be transported, such defects cannot be discovered until the next day when inspection takes place. For example, if defects occur early in the morning it would require a long time for defects to be discovered, allowing more defects to be produced in large quantities posing serious damage[2] to the company.

To avoid this, defects must be discovered as early as possible and resolved. The best method to achieve this is conducting inspection right after each product is manufactured.

---

2 Wasting raw materials and the labor that was spent on making defective and unsold items. Serious damages include wasting raw materials, production time, and so on.

However, it is a fact that transporting each finished product to the inspection department would be cumbersome.

Another alternative is to bring inspectors to final production and perform inspections on the shop floor. The problem would surely be solved with this method and will most certainly allow defects to be discovered in no time. However, it is given that inspectors will show strong resistance to this idea. They may complain about having to perform inspections in the busy environment of the shop floor instead of in the quiet and familiar environment of their laboratories.

PURCHASING DEPARTMENT AND DESIGN DEPARTMENT
"PROSPECTIVE NEW PRODUCTS BUT SUPPLIERS NEED TO BE CHANGED"

Workers often become excited about releases of new products and additional profit gains. However, workers in the purchasing department may not be as excited upon learning details of a new product. For example, if a new product is not much different from the previous version in terms of specifications, but is quite different in terms of design, it may require an entirely different group of components that need to be supplied from completely different suppliers.

Assume that this company has succeeded in purchasing components through the use of Kanbans; it has taken the company a great deal of effort to do so. They spent a tremendous amount of time in explaining the virtues of the Toyota System and Kanbans not only to their own factories, but also to their suppliers. They made sure that Pick-up Logistics Service was running effectively, and went as far as visiting their suppliers to make sure that they were well-prepared to manage incoming Kanbans.

However, their tremendous efforts were reduced to naught, as different suppliers were designated for producing new products. They would have to repeat the same training to new suppliers.

94

In developing new products, designers attempt to implement a design that reduces production cost as much as possible[3]. This is why new suppliers were selected to supply less expensive components. However, it is never smart to change components just because of its lower price.

TECHNICAL DEPARTMENT AND PRODUCTION DEPARTMENT
"STOP THAT SELF-MANUFACTURING!"

Continuous improvement can streamline a process to where work once done by 10 workers can be done by eight. This means that productivity of two workers has been freed up. These two workers are assigned to a task of self-manufacturing[4] components that have been purchased from suppliers. The components had been provided by suppliers as they had the necessary technologies and labor to produce them, and the factory did not. After serious consideration, the factory reached the conclusion that it was feasible to assign the two freed workers to manufacture the components with their improved technologies. Self-manufacturing the components turned out to be more hassle than they had expected. They finally became successful in self-manufacturing the components after 3 months of trial and error.

Samples of the components were sent to the technical department to obtain final approval for the components to be utilized in production. Instead of giving a result, though, the technical department kept asking the question of why the components needed to be self-manufactured, given that there was nothing wrong with purchasing them from suppliers.

They were quite hesitant to give approval, and gave an excuse for their disapproval. They claimed that self-manufacturing would only increase production cost and decrease profitability. The Technical Department should be supportive

3 Designers who come up with the most cost effective design are highly valued.
4 Instead of outsourcing production to suppliers, the production is carried out within the factory in order to minimize the cost of production.

toward the shop floor at all times. However, in this case, it was doing nothing but getting in the way of the shop floor.

Factory Shop Floor and Sales Representatives
"What sales representatives say should not be trusted"

"Please come into the factory and prepare these products... I received orders from a very important customer of mine . . ." A request like this from sales representatives are frequently given to factory workers. One factory worker even had the experience of having to cancel a visit the zoo with his children and come to work on the weekend.

In the past, finished products were transported from factories to distribution centers on a daily basis. However, with reduced amount of inventories to maintain, factories started to notice empty space in storage after the Toyota System was introduced. Factories also became capable of reducing production time so that products could be delivered to customers in a timely manner. This also allowed factories to ship products directly from their facilities to customers instead of storing finished products in distribution centers. When products were transported back from distribution centers to the factory, workers were frustrated to see the abundance of finished products for which they had to sacrifice their weekends to keep customers satisfied.

Accounting Department and Factory Shop Floor
"Ignore sales trends when conducting production!"

One day, the factory received a request from the accounting department. It demanded the factory to manufacture items as previously planned, regardless of sales trends, instead of producing the only items in quantities indicated by sales orders.

This would significantly increase their inventories. In

96

fact, the factory had overhauled its new production system. They went from relying heavily on inaccurate sales forecasts to producing items on sales demand by effectively shortening production time. The last thing they hoped to do was to increase the volume of inventories by granting the request from the accounting department. The accounting department was asked the logic behind their request and were told that management had judged that profits would continue to go down as inventories kept shrinking in size.

The shop floor workers had a hard time accepting this answer. The fact that reducing inventories could lead to a loss of profit did not make sense at all. Promoters of the Toyota System would become completely lost upon learning that every accomplishment by the Toyota System needed to be reversed.

Who can resolve conflicts between these different departments?

As described in the examples, implementation of the Toyota System can cause conflicts, distrustfulness, and suspicions among departments within a company. These conflicts cannot be resolved only by having negotiations between directors of each department, as they often focus on the benefit of their own department. They also do their best not to accept any changes that are disadvantageous to their team. So, who can reconcile these conflicts? It is done by the top executives of a company.

5-2 Caught in the Accounting System Trap

HOW MUCH PROFIT CAN BE EXPECTED THIS YEAR?

I am going to give you a small calculation exercise. Please think about it for a minute.

> *Problem* - Bicycle frame manufacturer, Takada Metal, purchased components for $12 million to cover manufacturing their yearly production goal, which required 2,400 components. $12 million was also spent on labor to produce the frames. In fact, they sold frames (equal to 2,000 components) with a gross sales of $30 million. How much profit did they make in this scenario?

Figure 34: Profit Gain Equation I

HOW SHOULD IT BE CALCULATED?

Those who simply subtracted the costs of the components and labor from the gross sales profit end up with inaccurate answers.

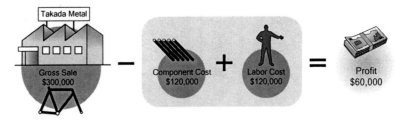

Figure 35: Profit Gain Equation 2

The cost of components to be subtracted from the gross profit should be $10 million dollars instead of $12 million, since only 2,000 components were used, even though 2,400 components had been purchased originally.

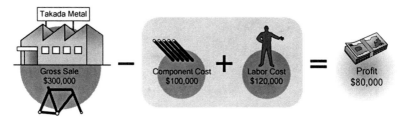

Figure 36: Correct Profit Gain Equation

Does it make sense to you? This calculation can be either accurate, or inaccurate, depending on the situation. I will explain this in detail in the next sections.

The actual production cost depends on the production volume

It is actually a tricky question to solve, simply because adding the cost of the components and labor to calculate the net profit[5] does not equal the actual production cost. In other words, the actual production cost to be used for calculating the net profit is determined by how many components were actually used to produce the frames.

Let me explain how the actual production cost can be calculated when the amount of manufactured frames vary while using components in the quantities of 2,000, 2,200 and 2,400.

The cost of components is determined upon purchasing

In terms of the cost of components per frame, the cost is determined at the time of purchase. The components were pur-

---

5 If the amount of raw material purchased, and that of raw materials used for actual production, as well as the amount of produced items and that of sold items, are different, then the cost of actual production can be calculated by using the number of items that are actually sold. In this example, the actual costs of raw materials and labor can be calculated by using 2,000 components used for production.

chased for $12 million to produce the necessary number of frames (2,400).

The cost per frame can be calculated by;

Figure 37: Component Cost per Frame

No matter how many frames are produced, such as 2,000, 2,200 or 2,400, the cost per frame remains $5,000.

In a case where 2,000 frames are sold, the actual total material component cost to sales can be calculated as follows:

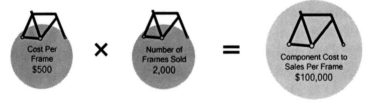

Figure 38: Material Component Cost to Sales

The same cost per frame is also used to calculate other residual costs associated with unsold finished frames and leftover materials.

Fluctuating labor cost

Labor cost is also taken into consideration for calculating the actual production cost to sales and that of unsold frames. However, labor cost is not included in the cost of materials.

Thus, the labor cost per frame is calculated by dividing the total labor cost by the number of produced frames. Then, it is applied independently to calculate the actual production cost to sales and the cost of unsold frames. These costs are greatly influenced by the overall production volume.

Full-time factory workers usually operate under fixed salaries. This means that, no matter how many more products are to be manufactured, the labor cost will not increase as long as products are completed in a fixed amount of time. Therefore, the labor cost per frame decreases as more frames are produced in a fixed amount of time, which leads to reduction in the actual production cost.

Labor cost associated with unsold frames that are not included in the actual production cost to sales in a certain year will be included in calculating the actual production cost to sales for the following year.

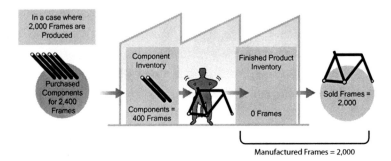

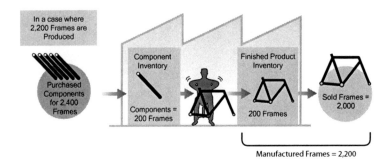

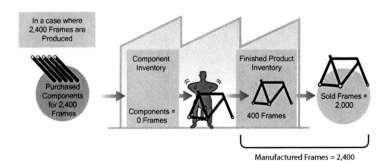

Figure 39: Manufactured Frames vs. Frames Sold

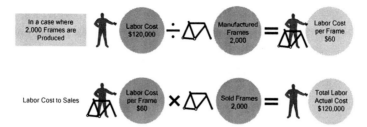

Labor cost associated with finished product inventory is zero because such an inventory does not exist in this case.

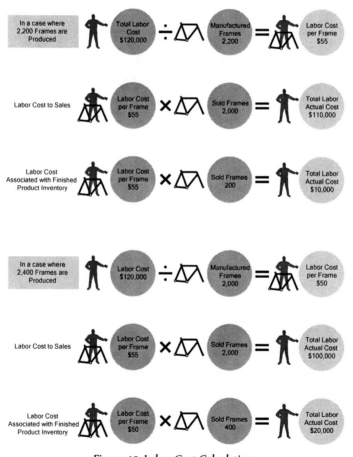

Figure 40: Labor Cost Calculations

The correct answer cannot be determined unless we know the production volume, as that determines how the total labor cost can be distributed to calculate the actual production cost and the cost of unsold frames.

To make this clear, let me explain how the net profit can be calculated separately when different numbers of frames are produced using 2,000, 2,200 and 2,400 components.

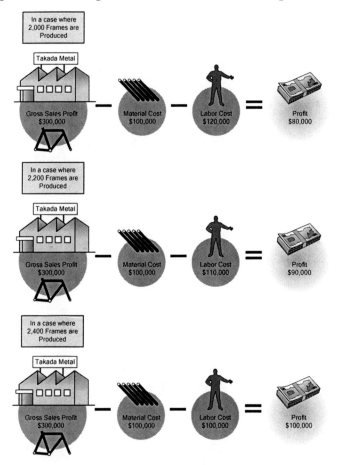

Figure 41: Production Volume Determines Net Profit

As illustrated in the figure, more net profit can be generated as more production output is yielded. An increase in profit is always gratifying. It is an ideal manufacturing system where profits are boosted exponentially by increasing production output and sales, while reducing the actual production cost at the same time.

As for the answer to the question in this chapter, the net profit can be easily shifted from $8 to $10 million depending on the production volume. However, the accounting system still calculated $10 million as the maximum attainable profit.

On the other hand, a serious problem could occur if the sales plunged while the production volume was kept high to reduce the actual production cost. Unsold items would obviously be left in the inventory for a period of time. However, it is not an issue in accounting because the remaining items in stock can be sold in the future. Even if sales do not pick up, factories would continue to produce in large quantities and maintain the inventory of unsold items in order to maintain the lower overall production cost. In short, the larger the inventory becomes, the more profit can be generated in the end.

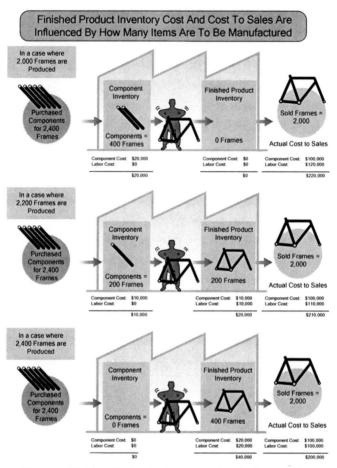

Figure 42: Finished Production Inventory Cost & Cost to Sales is Influenced by How Many Items are Manufactured

RISKS ASSOCIATED WITH INVENTORY

It would not be problematic as long as items continue to be sold even after being stored in inventory for a short period of time. However, new products are constantly introduced on the market these days, and products experience a much faster turnover. In other words, if a product is over produced factories are most likely to have to deal with unsold items.

If items remain unsold, the following disadvantages can be observed:

1. Cost associated with disposing inventory.
2. Cost associated with maintaining inventory until it can be disposed of completely.
3. Overall production cost may exceed the calculated profit in accounting (Extraordinary Loss Treatment).

As for (1) and (2), they simply cause more undesirable cash spending and affect the entire cash flow[6] of the company in a negative manner. As for (3), profit becomes questionable as production cost is calculated to be unexpectedly high. This kind of situation is referred to as "Extraordinary Loss Treatment," which focuses on continuing production while focusing on maximizing profit by lowering production cost with no regards toward how products may sell. As a result, unsold products and their associated costs are taking their ironic turn to reduce profit.

TRICKS TO MAKING SUPERFICIAL PROFITS

Most corporations conduct business with funds that are collected from their stockholders. Therefore, meetings with stock holders take place regularly to disclose profits earned by the company. If the results are not satisfactory to investors, management of the company is simply replaced. Yearly profit yield by the company is what investors are most interested in. Therefore, companies try their best on a daily basis to maximize their sales profits and limit production costs until it is time to announce results to the public.

Profits should be expanded, essentially, by making more sales through the consistent efforts of sales representatives, while factories continue to implement continuous improvements to reduce production costs. However, as I have illus-

6 It also means the financial revenue that remains within a company after costs of materials and labor are subtracted from gross revenue.

trated up to this point, production costs can be lowered if production continues to take place without any regard to how products sell on the market. Unfortunately, many companies choose this method and present superficial profits for the purpose of keeping their investors satisfied.

Who can take decisive steps toward increasing profits?

No matter how dedicated factories become in their effort toward eliminating inventory by adopting the Toyota System, the top management always has authority to put a hold on any new strategies if they find it to be ineffective towards maximizing profits.

Therefore, it ultimately depends on the top management to decide which production method is most suitable. Options are either to keep producing unmarketable goods to yield superficial profits while suffering from inventories simply to reduce production costs (a short-term perspective) or to avoid producing unmarketable goods and eliminating inventories even though production costs may stay high and profits are not always guaranteed (a long-term perspective).

5-3 The Top Management only gives commands and nothing else

What are the roles of the top management?

As the Toyota System optimizes an entire company as a whole, instead of selectively improving the shop floor, various conflicts between departments and contradictions within a certain production system, including accounting systems, can be witnessed.

Improvement efforts toward a comprehensive optimization may give advantages to certain departments and other departments may suffer from unfavorable results. This kind of problem can never be dealt with by any solutions formulated by section leaders or department chiefs. Only clear and specific instructions from the top management can solve such problems.

By the way, the top executives are usually very busy in general and may not have the necessary means to deliver the most effective solutions. Is it really good enough if the top management comes into the game only when these conflicts and contradictions occur?

In the past, there was not enough information pertaining to the Toyota System available so that we could teach ourselves about the system. Only a handful of manuals and self-proclaimed Toyota consultants had the knowledge to share, and some of the results we had witnessed were questionable. However, now there are various types of literature addressing the Toyota System which have become abundant in bookstores in recent years. Also, the invention of the internet has helped us acquire an endless flow of information by simply looking up the words, "Toyota System."

In addition, many companies outside the Toyota Group have provided us with their successful stories of implementing the Toyota System on their shop floors, which has allowed us to develop a further understanding of the Toyota System. Moreover, many retirees of Toyota who studied the Toyota System under Taiichi Ohno have made themselves available to companies that are willing to learn. Those companies have experienced a high rate of success in incorporating the Toyota System into their production systems.

As I mentioned, it has become much easier to attempt to implement the Toyota System in our workplaces as long as we become committed to learning about it. On the other hand, the top management may believe that the Toyota System can be easily adopted by inviting expert trainers, or reading and mimicking successful stories of other factories. However, this type of attitude will always remain an illusion. Successful implementation of the Toyota System remains extremely difficult if such underestimation continues.

ENTERTAINING CONSULTANTS SHOULD NOT BE A ROLE OF THE TOP MANAGEMENT

Most companies that are eager to adopt the Toyota System in the shortest amount of time often ask for the help of consultants. These consultants are either retirees of Toyota Group companies or from the companies that had already succeeded in adopting the Toyota System.

Every such consultant demands the top management to take the leadership roles in implementing the Toyota System. Some of the top management executives do actually manage to follow the instruction and step into the shop floor on a daily basis in spite of their busy schedule. This kind of commitment usually sends the shop floor workers a message that the company is serious about the Toyota System and its potential outcome.

On the other hand, other top management executives choose not to invest their time and effort at all. They may not visit the shop floor at all or visit only in the beginning of the long implementation process. They may show up in the factory only when the consultant shows up for trainings on the shop floor. They may also show up only in board rooms to meet with consultants and leave to entertain consultants as soon as meetings are over.

The shop floor workers and section leaders witness these behaviors of the top management and develop suspicions that their time and effort will be wasted repeatedly to achieve no results whatsoever. The worst case would be when they lose their interests in trying harder, as they have seen many other consultants who had failed to train on quality control, industrial engineering, or whatever topics that happened to be popular at the time.

In some cases, the top management only manage to make themselves available once a week to receive a new set of instructions from consultants. A consultant usually visits every part of the shop floor to make sure that his instructions were carried out since his last visit. The top management usually tours with the consultant and are eager to learn any progress made by new, continuous improvement methods. In the past, training with consultants would begin and complete in a meeting room with more paper work to deal with at the end. But, training for the Toyota System takes place on the shop floor so that the actual problems can be witnessed and effective solutions can be formulated at the actual place. Any improvement made on the shop floor over a given period is carefully evaluated and new instructions are given after conducting FAQ sessions among workers in order to ensure their clear understanding toward the next improvement goals. It is clear that those who do not visit the shop floor frequently have no idea what progress is being made. What is worse is that such top management executives fail to remember what instructions were given by the consultant and need to be constantly reminded by other workers on the shop floor. When they finally remember, it gets worse. They may start to furiously complain and blame the workers if instructions were not met on the day before the consultants show up.

Shop floor workers will always find it incredibly frustrating to see the top management acting as if they were consultants themselves. This example is surely far from being the ideal situation, in which the top management fails to proactively take the leadership in continuous improvement challenges.

In most cases, positive results can certainly be obtained if the shop floor workers properly follow instructions from consultants and continue to work hard towards continuous improvements. However, in the process of conducting continuous improvement methods, the shop floor workers often run into problems that cannot be resolved either by their capacities or instructions from consultants.

For example, the processing department is most likely to suffer from such a situation. It is much harder for the processing department to produce only the necessary items in the right quantity in the right time, than it is for the assembly department. Workers in assembly need to perform changeovers of machinery in order to produce different types of products in a flow. To achieve that, it is extremely important for the processing department to shorten the changeover time in order to minimize time and labor required for production.

However, it is always a challenge to shorten changeover times. The shop floor workers often feel devastated when they are ordered to perform 10 changeovers everyday within 10 minute allowance for each changeover. Especially when they had to perform only one changeover per a day within a one hour allowance previously.

Progress should be made on a step by step basis in order to achieve the final goals on the horizon. The same rule can be applied to working toward continuous improvements. If the shop floor workers are ordered to deliver positive results in an unreasonable amount of time, they often have a tendency to simply give up without even trying, or show resistance to any new changes to their conventional methods.

Even though it is a good idea to have consultants giving out instructions on a regular basis, the top management should not be scolding the shop floor workers every time workers fail to yield the desired results. Otherwise, the shop workers will be fed up with their incompetent superiors and become disengaged from the whole process. In most cases where the top management only shows up on the shop floor on the day of and prior to the training by consultants, despite the fact that the top management initiated the whole consulting process, the shop floor workers begin to behave in the same manner as anyone can expect.

NEGLIGENCE AND THE LACK OF UNDERSTANDING FROM THE TOP MANAGEMENT LEADS TO A DISSIMULATION WITHIN CONTINUOUS IMPROVEMENT ACTIVITIES

Many challenges must be overcome in adopting the Toyota System into production. The motivation of the shop floor workers would be greatly diminished if top management imposed full responsibilities without assistance, and blame the lack of commitment on workers if continuous improvement methods fail.

However, workers are obligated to follow instructions from their superiors whether they like it or not. In some cases, workers stage the shop floor so that the given instructions look as if they had been carried out when consultants revisit the shop floor for inspection. Some workers go as far as manipulating the progress reports so that only the favorable results are presented to the top management.

In cases where workers become concentrated upon dissimulating the shop floor, even the president of a company is led to believe that the Toyota System has been successfully implemented in his factories. Even when workers are instructed to conduct production according to Kanbans, they choose not to follow and end up suffering from the excessive left over items on the shop floor while additional Kanbans continue flowing in. Such excessive items are transported to a storage space to keep hidden from consultants in a few days prior to inspection. Of course, consultants are not like presidents and will not be deceived so easily. They would never overlook any unnecessary items left laying on the shop floor.

Such a dissimulation on the shop floor is quite labor intensive. If excessive items have already been assembled, it would be extremely cumbersome to hide them in a strange place and bring them back to the assembly lines. In this situation, it is reasonable to say that the Toyota System brings more unnecessary work to the shop floor rather than working toward increasing efficiency in production.

SUCCESS OF THE TOYOTA SYSTEM IS DICTATED BY MANAGEMENT, NOT THE SHOP FLOOR

Most companies that attempt to overcome their management crisis by the Toyota System are often lead by responsible top management. The shop floor workers determine the likelihood of success by measuring how committed the top management is to the whole implementation process.

When working toward implementing the Toyota System, it is critical for companies that are fortunate enough not to have confronted a management crisis, to stay on alert because financial crisis may come to haunt them in the near future. A great deal of resistance against new changes can be experienced in such a company, especially when profits are currently generated to exceed their expectations. For such a reason, the top management must take decisive actions so that the resistance to new changes can be removed from the shop floor workers.

Top management which chooses not take proactive roles may present such excuses as "I don't know anything about factories since I worked as a sales person" or "I have no idea how products are actually manufactured, as I have worked only as a product designer in the past. That's why I put the shop floor in charge of achieving continuous improvement in production." These excuses may be valid to a certain degree but often lead the shop floor workers to question the commitment of the top management toward implementing the Toyota System.

If the top management is lacking the knowledge of manufacturing or factory mechanisms, they must willingly start studying the Toyota System on their own. This way they will be able to fully understand what the Toyota System entails and how it should be practiced in the most effective manner by taking a leadership role in the whole process.

In addition, the Toyota System does alter the methods of production one way or another. Workers may become concerned as the initial results may not be substantial, but remain ambiguous for a while as new changes are being introduced, and new tasks are performed on the shop floor. However, instead of constantly applying pressure on workers to not make mistakes, top management should focus their efforts on successfully adopting new changes on the shop floor, and helping workers overcome new problems by formulating effective solutions along the way. This is the essence of what being a part of top management is all about. Only top management can overcome these challenges.

As I stated, the top management must always broadcast the message of showing invincible determination towards the Toyota System by their own behaviors. If they fail to do so, the shop floor workers will lose their commitment and face a series of failures while hoping the "Epidemic of the Toyota System" among the top management will eventually become of no importance. I cannot stress enough that whether or not the Toyota System becomes successful, the success of our factories are heavily dictated by the degree of commitment from the top management.

6. THE TRUE METHODS OF PRACTICING THE TOYOTA SYSTEM

6-1 The Toyota System is a New Religion

WHY IS IMPLEMENTATION OF THE TOYOTA SYSTEM NOT SUCCESSFUL?

Terminologies found in books and literature of the Toyota System such as "Just–in–Time," "Kanban System," and "Ji-doka" can be difficult to comprehend at first, but become easier to understand after obtaining some useful explanations. However, many shop floors have experienced either no positive results at all, or only the adverse effects in some cases.

I have illustrated in this book various examples in which the implementation of the Toyota System has failed. This is not to explain that the Toyota System is so complex that it cannot be comprehended by ordinary people, but is to describe situations where people — not the system — failed. Even though they thought it possible to achieve the results they needed, there were always specific reasons for the cause of failure. I have described the importance of the role of top management and the total optimization of production. In this chapter, I am going to review the fundamental principles of the Toyota System from the previous chapters in the context of trying to explain the reasons why the Toyota System can lead to undesirable results.

Most importantly, the Toyota System requires us to change the basic mechanism of our conventional production systems. Utilizing only the tools such as the Kanban System will not help us achieve the desirable results in the long run. Advantages of Kanbans cannot be reaped unless the basic manufacturing process is revised and is continuously improved over time. Some people may argue that the desired results can be attained as long as continuous improvement efforts are made consistently on the shop floor. However, it is not as simple as that due to the unique nature of the Toyota System. This is what sets it apart from any other production system from the past.

In this sense, the fact that the Toyota System is so unique requires us to have a totally different way of thinking toward manufacturing. In fact, removing ourselves from our old habits and submerging ourselves into the mind-set of the Toyota System is the biggest challenge we will need to overcome during the implementation process.

DIFFERENCE FROM THE CONVENTIONAL PRODUCTION SYSTEM #1
"PRODUCTION OUTPUT IS DRASTICALLY REDUCED"

Conventional production system: "Produce and transport items in batch."

Traditionally, it is often considered that it is more cost-effective to produce items in batch as much as possible. Batch processes do not require any irregularity in how work is performed and the time need for changeovers is greatly reduced[1] if a certain type of item is continuously produced.

The Toyota System: "Producing and transporting items diligently creates a flow in production"

The secret is to keep everything at a minimum. It means that items are produced for only the quantity sold previously. For example, if one item is sold, we limit production to produce only one item to replace the sold one. It does not have to be as low as one item at a time, but the idea is that the smaller the quantity, the more efficient production becomes under the Toyota System.

The same rule can be applied to items that need to be transported diligently as they are being produced. Even if we manage to produce items one by one but still transport the items in batch, no progress has been made and it is still considered batch processing. Efficiency can only be gained when a smaller number of items are transported each time.

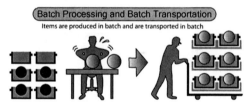

Figure 43: Batch Processing and Transportation

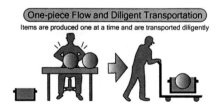

Figure 44: One-piece Flow and Diligent Transportation

---

1 Workers often need to juggle between different screwdrivers to put in certain screws. Many changeovers are required to maintain one-piece flow production. On the other hand, batch processing does not need changeovers, allowing workers to shorten production time.

DIFFERENCE FROM THE CONVENTIONAL PRODUCTION SYSTEM #2
"PRODUCTION INSTRUCTIONS ARE ESSENTIALLY DIFFERENT"

Conventional production system: "Production is scheduled in advance."

In a conventional production system, the shop floor workers start their daily work according to predetermined production schedules. Such schedules also indicate the necessary work to be performed for the days following tomorrow[2]. This still allows workers to batch process items on a given day as long as they are the same items that are scheduled to be produced over the week.

The Toyota System: "Process only the items ordered by the post processes."

The shop floor produces only the items to replace the sold items in the necessary quantity. Post processes frequently give instructions to the shop floor to achieve that. In this manner, the shop floor workers are not given any definite production plan as to what needs to be processed each day, which disables any batch processing in advance. In other words, workers learn what needs to be processed on a case by case basis[3].

---

2 In many cases, the shop floor workers receive set schedules for one week at a time.
3 Workers may become concerned with having to shift from having predetermined schedules to not knowing until instructions are received. Continuous improvement must be put in place so that they feel comfortable with this new method.

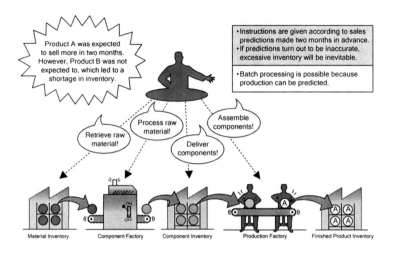

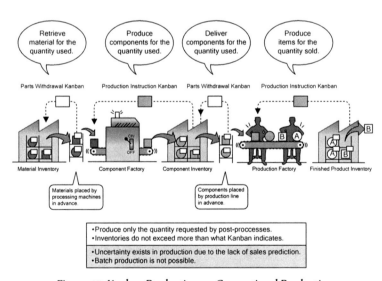

Figure 45: Kanban Production vs. Conventional Production

DIFFERENCE FROM THE CONVENTIONAL PRODUCTION SYSTEM #3
DIFFERENT APPROACHES TO CONTINUOUS IMPROVEMENT

> Conventional production system: "Partial optimization is encouraged."

Conventional production systems maximize profit by achieving partial optimizations in selected portions of production. Profit is also maximized by purchasing components and producing items at the lowest costs possible. When components are purchased in batch, the cost per component becomes significantly lower. In the same respect, if items are produced in larger quantities the production costs associated with labor and equipment amortization per product can be lowered as well. Unsold items are kept in inventory until they become marketable through market demand in the future.

> The Toyota System: "Total Optimization is strongly encouraged."

In order to achieve the total optimization of manufacturing processes, removing wastes from each department, including sales, production, and purchasing, is often prioritized for the purpose of reducing production cost. To achieve elimination of wastes, production systems need to be redesigned so that items can be purchased when they are needed in the necessary quantities. Items should not be produced more than the quantity sold to avoid overstocking the items. Overstock is considered a waste under the Toyota System.

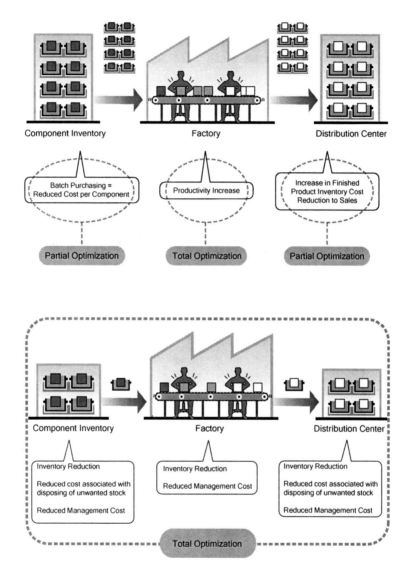

Figure 46: Toyota System's Total Optimization

The Toyota System is a new religion for manufacturing processes

As I explained, the Toyota System seems to lack common sense from a perspective of what has been considered as normal in conventional production systems. It is similar to when the Buddhist Japanese became confused when Christianity was introduced to Japan.

In the same respect, a transition to a completely new production system can be almost impossible to achieve. In some cases, the beliefs and habits that are embedded through a conventional production system prevents us from achieving a flow in production under the Toyota System.

By the way, the concept of "a flow in production" is challenging for us to grasp in a practical sense. I will explain this more in detail by using an analogy of the flow of water in a river.

	Conventional System	Toyota System
Production Method	Batch Processing (Big waves / Tsunami)	One-Piece Flow (Ripple waves)
Instructions	Ordered by Set Schedules Schedules are sometimes inaccurate and hard to comply with	Ordered by Post Processes When sales drops, the flow is stopped.
Continuous Improvement Strategy	Partial Optimization	Total Optimization
	No Flow	Flow

Figure 47: Toyota System vs. Conventional Production Flow

6-2 A Flow in Production

LIKE THE FLOW OF PURE WATER

The Kanban System and the Toyota System are essentially different from one another. Kanban System is a management method, whereas the Toyota System is the fundamental mechanism of manufacturing itself. Productions that operate under the Toyota System essentially accommodate a flow in production in the simplest form and, without such a flow, the Kanban System will likely fail.

The analogy of river flow is often used to better explain a flow in production. Of course, there are many different types of a flow such as those found in stagnate rivers in urban areas, placid streams in deep mountains, rivers covered by concrete walls and so on. These rivers accommodate the same kind of flow of water, but the flow of a placid streams is most suitable for explaining the Toyota System, as it maintains a flow of pure water without an end.

The flow of placid streams is maintained by ice melt and rainfall, it never ceases to exist, even on a sunny day. This is because the flow is maintained by the two sources of water, that flow in from the mountains.

TO MAINTAIN A FLOW IN THE RIVER

Rivers experience a shift in flow as heavy rains or droughts occur. In some cases, the absence of the flow of pure water causes a clouding of the water. If a river suffers from cloudiness on the banks, this causes serious damage to the surrounding natural habitat and people who are dependant on the water for life.

If this type of problem occurs, people often artificially attempt to regenerate the flow by removing sludge or paving the river bottom with concrete. However, these efforts may not be sufficient to prevent additional flooding or droughts, as extreme whether conditions can never be predicted. This is why people build dams upstream so that the volume of water can be carefully adjusted with ease. In the end, stabilizing the flow by using these efforts will eventually lead to safer living for people downstream and around the river.

To Create a Flow in Factory Settings

How can we generate a flow in production as far as factories are concerned? As for the river, water flows from upstream to downstream indefinitely. In other words, it flows from a higher elevation to a lower elevation.

On the other hand, neither purchased raw materials nor components in a factory transport themselves. They need to be transported by forklifts from one storage place to another or one process to another. Therefore, transporting items continuously is critical if the flow has to be generated in a factory setting.

By the way, the Toyota System defines 7 categories of wastes to be removed from production. One of those wastes pertains to wastes associated with "unnecessary transportation." Some people may argue that it is less wasteful to process and transport items in batch. However, what happens to the flow in production if processed items are constantly held so that they can be transported by batch later? A flow becomes visible only when items are being transported and it ceases to exist when items arrive at their destination. It is just like a river whose flow is inconsistent due to heavy rainfall and droughts.

So how do we create this flow? It is effectively accomplished by transporting items diligently instead of by batch. Using this method causes concern for some people because transporting items so frequently leads to more waste by requiring more workers than needed. Such concerns can be eliminated by formulating effective solutions that will maintain a flow and does not lead to an increase in labor.

One of the solutions is to alter the shop floor layout, which simplifies transportation and allows workers to travel the shortest distances. The Toyota System designates "Water Spiders" to perform all the necessary transportation tasks on the shop floor. In such a case, the efficiency of "Water Spiders" is continuously improved to be more efficient as well.

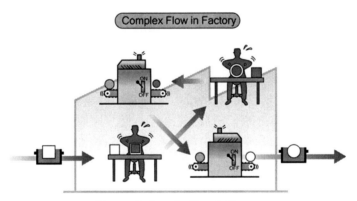

Figure 48: Complex Flow in Factory

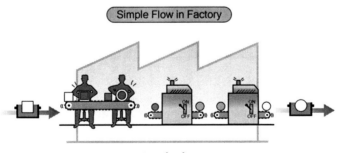

Figure 49: Simple Flow in Factory

Batch processing at any point in production hinders the creation of flow even when items are transported diligently from one process to another. If batch processing continues, there would not be enough items to be transported frequently.

For example, when it takes one second to process a certain item, it takes one minute to produce 60 items. If it takes more than one hour to process an item, 60 hours are required to process 60 items. This is extremely problematic if transportation only occurs once a week, stopping the flow for more than one week at a time. It can still be viewed as a flow if items are transported every hour. However, a flow simply ceases to exist when items are transported only once every week. What can be done to solve this?

The answer is to process items one by one[4] instead of to produce items by batch. The shop floor layout needs to be reformatted to accommodate this method so that production time can be significantly reduced. The cell production system is conceptualized based on this principle.

---

4 This is called "One-piece Flow."

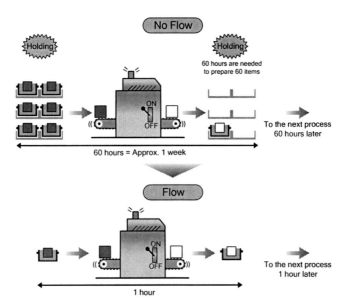

Figure 50: Production Flow vs. No Flow

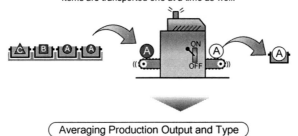

Figure 51: Averaging Production Output of Mixed Items

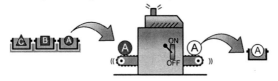

PRODUCE MULTIPLE KINDS OF ITEMS AT THE SAME TIME

We have looked at flow production where the same type of items are continuously processed. Now let us look at processes in which mixed items are processed. Going back to the analogy of a river flow, a river consists of many tributary streams that eventually connect together downstream to become one unified river. A clog in the smallest tributary stream can cause a drought downstream.

This analogy can be applied to manufacturing. Production flow cannot be stabilized if only one kind of item is being produced constantly. Production flow on a larger scale can be achieved only when a mix of various kinds of items are simultaneously produced.[5] Processing one unit of product A, one unit of product B, and one unit of product C would be a good example of this method.

ONE-PIECE PRODUCTION AND DILIGENT TRANSPORTATION REDUCE THE PRODUCTION TIME AND INVENTORY

One-piece production and diligent transportation of items creates a flow in production that significantly reduces the production time as a result. The Conventional production method often stores both processed and unprocessed items all over the shop floor in large quantities. These excessive items were being held until they were transported to the next process, or were simply waiting for their turns to be processed. This was because items were batch processed and transported in lots.

In such cases, even if the processing time for each component was kept short, the production time ended up being many days or weeks as every item faced a long holding time until it was moved onto the next process. Additionally, the factory could still be batch producing 100 units of product A and product B respectively, even if a sales representative

5 Processing multiple kinds of items at the same time is called "Mixed Production."

asked for only one of each to be delivered. In this case, the shop floor wastes labor and time for processing the remaining 99 units for each product, which did not get sold. The remaining items may be sold in the future. If not, it is the factory that will suffer from excessive inventories.

In contrast, if items are processed by one-piece flow and transported frequently, the total production time can be drastically reduced from weeks to only a few days or hours. Furthermore, maintaining a flow while averaging production enables the shop floor to accommodate unique demands and requirements from post-processes — including sales representatives and assembly departments.

As I explained, averaging items in production while maintaining a flow influences the surroundings in a positive manner. Without a flow, preceding processes may have to store more items than necessary so that requests from post processes can be accommodated at any given time. This implies a great risk of having to maintain a large volume of overstocked inventory. Therefore, production flow must carefully be maintained so that inventories can be minimized and requests from post process become equalized.

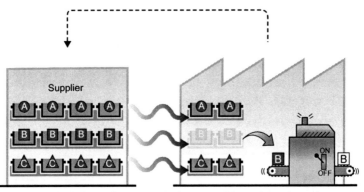

Inventories for A, B, and C are excessively
maintained to avoid shortages.

B is continuously used
up first. Then, A and C.

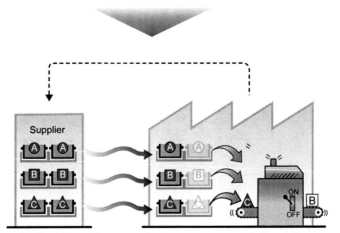

Inventories for A, B, and C can be maintained
in low volume. Each type of item is equally
demanded by post processes.

A, B, and C are
equally used.

Figure 52: Flow in Production

6-3 Steps for Implementing the Toyota System

CREATING A FLOW IN PRODUCTION IS THE FIRST THING TO DO

As I have explained so far, various adverse effects and frustrations among workers will be the end result if the Toyota System is applied with an inappropriate perception of its key principles and methodologies. The Toyota System is essentially a method for creating an ideal manufacturing system. Utilizing only Kanbans does not lead to success in its implementation. To make sure that the Toyota System functions in the most desirable way, a flow in production must be achieved and is systemized by applying available tools such as the Kanban System.

A flow in production can be achieved by:

Step 1: "Creating a flow in every process"

Step 2: "Incorporating the mechanism of "Just–in–Time"

Step 3: "Practicing endless continuous improvement efforts (it should be carried out repeatedly after going back to Step 1)"

After a flow in production is realized to some degree, the mechanism of "Just–in–Time" should be incorporated into production. A successful adoption of "Just–in–Time" does not mean the end of the whole process. Every step must be carried out repeatedly so that the shop floor continues to be improved to solidify the flow in production. I will explain each step in detail in the following sections.

6-4 Step 1: "Creating a Flow in Every Process"

CHANGING THE SHOP FLOOR LAYOUT TO OBTAIN THE "SHORTEST DISTANCES"

The key to a successful implementation of "Just–in–Time" is creating a flow in every process. Let me explain how a flow can be formulated in factory settings.

Let us visualize driving a car in the city. If streets meander or are filled with parked cars, you will not be able to drive smoothly or, in some cases, will run into a traffic jam. This analogy can be applied to a factory environment. If the shop floor has a complex floor layout or components are stored excessively, the items can not be transported frequently no matter how much effort is put into sustaining one-piece flow. It would be time consuming and cumbersome for workers to transport items diligently as they need to dodge obstructions on their way. If storage spaces (parking lots, in the analogy above) for each item are not clearly identifiable, workers become incapable of easily identifying the necessary items and begin storing components in the right places.

To solve this type of situation, factories must carry out the 5S's, especially "Sorting" and "Set in Order" so that transportation routes become clearly visible with identifiable storage spaces. The shortest distance among work cells must be created to maximize transit efficiency.

Continuous improvement within production to promote one-piece flow

After the streets are maintained, the next thing to focus on is the method of transportation. Since large trucks need to sit until they are fully loaded, factories should use versatile motor bikes or smaller trucks so that they can ensure that items are being transported as a flow. In addition, continuous improvement principles such as "Production Line Improvement," "Set-up Time Improvement," and "Standardized Operation" are the most important methods for achieving one-piece flow operation.

"Production Line Improvement" aims at processing one item at a time — or in the smallest batch, with the greatest deal of efficiency, by eliminating wastes from workers and rearranging work tables to ensure items and tools are stored in the right places.

"Set-up Time Improvement" aims at shortening the time required for interchanging tools in machinery and swapping components so that multiple kinds of items can be processed and assembled simultaneously.

"Standardized Operation" aims at realizing a production mechanism in which workers are assigned to appropriate machinery to process items efficiently and repeat their assigned tasks so that the quality of each product can be carefully maintained.

EXTRA LABOR AND TIME ARE REQUIRED TO MAINTAIN PROGRESS IN CONTINUOUS IMPROVEMENT

No worker can afford to pass time in a factory. Rather, many factory workers have become victims of corporate downsizing, in order to compete with foreign factories. As a result, in some cases the shop floor is run by outsourced workers so that the overall production cost can be reduced. Since such outsourced workers cannot be relied upon, many factories have experienced a lack of time to commit to continuous improvement activities towards achieving a total optimization within production.

Continuously improving production is certainly a challenge that requires extra labor and time. Hardworking efforts of the shop floor workers must be present. For example, even if one-piece flow is in place, waste in workers need to be further identified in an absolute way by redesigning work cells and improving how tools and components are stored. However, improvement activities are generally carried out after a daily workload within designated work hours is completed. Therefore, improvement activities often require factories to devote extra time and labor in performing Sorting, Set in Order and redesigning the floor layout and worktables. Our consistent efforts and a long-term vision will help us discover solutions to our problems on a fundamental level.

6-5 Step 2: Formulating the "Just–in–Time" Mechanism

CREATING A "JUST–IN–TIME" MECHANISM

After a flow in production is in place, the next thing is incorporating a "Just–in–Time" mechanism into production. As I explained in Chapter 2, "Just–in–Time" is carried out by two distinct methods: "Sequential Parts Withdrawal" [6] and "Post-replenishment System (Kanban System)."

In order to initiate the Kanban System, there are many things to accomplish first. It starts from sorting and setting the shop floor in order, improving delivery packaging of components[7] and finally convincing suppliers to accept Kanbans by explaining various benefits and advantages associated with their new system. In fact, there are many cases where factories or suppliers find Kanbans too difficult to deal with and suggest another alternative method of "Sequential Parts Withdrawal" in order to simulate "Just–in–Time." However, "Sequential Parts Withdrawal" poses a great risk of forcing suppliers to maintain excessive inventory and becomes burdensome if suppliers are not capable of meeting supply demands. Therefore, it is much better, especially in the beginning of implementing the Toyota System, to maintain a certain volume of inventory in your own factory and receive supplies for only the items being utilized from suppliers, which is also known as "Post-replenishment System (Kanban System)."

To incorporate a mechanism of "Just–in–Time" you must

---

6 A method in which no inventory is maintained in your own process. When needed, suppliers and preceding processes are ordered to deliver the necessary items within a few hours to one day.

7 The quantity and type of items contained in a package can be easily identified by using a standardized method of packaging as well as the packaging materials.

have the "Kanban System," "Water Spiders" and "Procurement System" in place in advance. The Kanban System basically equals the Post-replenishment System. "Water Spiders" create an efficient flow of traffic on the shop floor. Finally, "Procurement System" allows frequent deliveries of raw materials and components from suppliers according to the requests made by the shop floor.

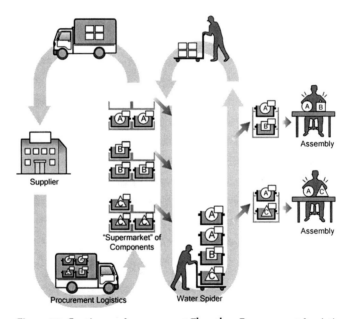

Figure 53: Continuous Improvement Flow thru Procurement Logistics

Production must be continuously improved so that an average production output can be sustained on a daily basis by one-piece flow. Improvement should also be made so that multiple types of products can be processed simultaneously. Since every item requires different components, "Water Spiders" are put in place to ensure efficient supplies of components to the shop floor.

A "supermarket" of components is established so that "Water Spiders" are able to retrieve only the necessary components in a timely manner. The floor layout of such a "supermarket" is carefully arranged, and components are stored in designated areas to allow easy withdrawals of components that are clearly labeled with Kanbans.

Another mechanism is created in a supermarket for restocking components that were removed from the inventory by "Water Spiders." When a Kanban is removed, it is brought back to suppliers so that the necessary components can be reordered. "Water Spiders" are also designated between factories and suppliers[8] to ensure a secure transit of Kanbans on a daily basis. Of course, suppliers need to be clearly instructed and trained on the true benefits to incorporating Kanbans into their supplying operations. Only when such agreements and arrangements are securely in place does the "Just–in–Time" System begin to be formulated into a successful production system.

BE CAUTIOUS OF ANY OPTIMISTIC IMPLEMENTATION OF I.T.

There are many other methods for transferring information to preceding processes besides Kanbans. In recent years, it has become possible to transfer data within a factory electronically without using any paper. The use of e–mails, especially, <u>has allowed us</u> to instantly complete our ordering processes.

8 "Water Spiders" between factories and suppliers are also called "Procurement Logistics" or "Milk Runners."

Inventory management is also performed by computers giving us the crucial information about inventory holdings as to what kinds of components are stored and where. It would be ideal if such computers could incorporate the functionality of Kanbans.

For example, in a case where 10 bicycles are to be produced, 10 frames are withdrawn from the component inventory and this information is entered into a computer. If a computer in preceding processes could receive this information and give instructions to process and supply 10 frames to the component inventory, it would perform the same functionality as Kanbans. Using actual Kanbans could be quite labor intensive as they need to be put on and removed from each item and handed over among departments. Using computers could save us time and labor to perform such cumbersome tasks. However, there is an all-too-common pitfall here.

Kanbans essentially allow us to perform maintenance by sight because they are always attached to the actual items. If each item in the inventory has a Kanban attached to it, it becomes much easier for workers to visualize if items are stocked sufficiently or not. Kanbans can also instruct exactly where certain items need to be stocked and how in terms of packaging.

On the other hand, if all such information is electronically maintained, it would be extremely difficult for workers to manage their inventory by sight unless they make every effort to manage it on the computer screen or print out every record. Continuous improvement also becomes less applicable on the shop floor and workers lose an effective way of exposing potential issues with the use of Kanbans. On a larger scale, it is obvious the Toyota System can fail to deliver its intended virtues, and factories end up simulating a Kanban-like system without achieving its true benefits. Due to these potential problems, the Toyota System should be implemented without any reliance on computers.

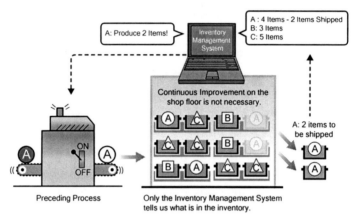

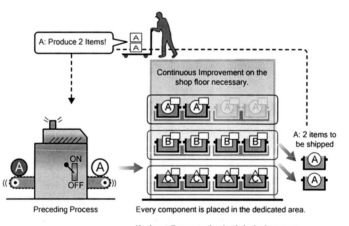

Figure 54: Visual Management vs. Virtual Management

6-6 Step 3: Remember that Continuous Improvement is a Never-ending Effort

NEVER PANIC IF YOU THINK YOU FAILED; UNSUCCESSFUL RESULTS ARE ALWAYS TO BE EXPECTED

Many unexpected results need to be dealt with as Kanban Systems are put into operation. Necessary components may not be transported as scheduled by preceding processes or may be delivered in wrong quantities. Production may not flow equally on a daily basis and inventories may not be minimized. "Water Spiders" may not be sufficient for distributing items in time. These are some examples of unexpected results you may encounter in the process.

You may jump the gun here and think that the Toyota System has completely failed. However, the very reason why it is not successful is that wastes have not been completely identified and eliminated within your production system, even when producing under the "Just–in–Time System." What you need to do is sustain your continuous improvement efforts so that such problems can be eliminated as you implement "Just–in–Time." Your efforts should focus not only on easily identifiable wastes that surface on the shop floor but also on specific wastes that are associated with the flow of production and the Kanban System itself, which goes one step further than simple waste identification. Such efforts should be constantly repeated. In addition, waste reduction is never complete, even when you assume that the Toyota System has accomplished your expected results. There is always room for further improvement that you may neither realize, nor expect. Let me give you some examples.

ELIMINATION OF WASTES HELP US FORMULATE THE NEXT GOAL FOR CONTINUOUS IMPROVEMENT

You should not be satisfied even when the inventory has been reduced by 60% (say the holding is reduced to one month from three months) by a flow in production and "Just-in-Time." What if the shop floor is still filled with excessive materials and components—especially near entrances or exits of the factory? It is true that continuous improvement alters the shop floor environment and brings about new changes. However, these may be just superficial outcomes of continuous improvement. By looking beyond these obvious results, we are able to identify various wastes that we had not been able to discover in the past.

A flow in production also needs to be established outside of your factory environment such as in suppliers and contractors. More wastes are most likely to be identified as the continuous improvement effort launches outward. In this manner, elimination of waste does not necessarily imply the end of your effort and you should not simply quit when the wastes are removed. Continuous improvement must be repeatedly carried out so that your immediate results become a stepping stone for you to achieve more meaningful and long-term improvement in production.

UNATTAINABLE GOALS MAKE IT POSSIBLE

When a consultant conducts training for the Toyota System, the shop floor is sometimes given uncompromising instructions to achieve on their own. If the Toyota System is to be implemented without the help of consultants, workers are required to have a much stronger commitment towards realizing such challenging goals.

For example, the shop floor is instructed to reduce the changeover time from one hour to 10 minutes to realize one-piece flow. Press machines[9] and injection molding machines[10] can easily take up to an hour to perform the changeover[11] with specific metal molds. Reducing it within 10 minutes is not an easy task. The shop may be able to manage to reduce the changeover time only by 10 to 20 minutes. However, the most important thing here is not to give up and try accomplishing what you can, one thing at a time. For the metal molds, start by sorting their storage space and put the most used molds closest to and the least used molds furthest away from your machinery. Metal molds should also stand by to be installed while machinery is in operation[12].

If we start with what we can do, we are often able to achieve much greater results than we would expect. The changeover time will be reduced significantly, if not within 10 minutes. Most people tend to become satisfied with the result being close enough to 10 minutes. However, the consultant is not usually satisfied here and demands the changeover time to be half. As long as we keep improving production in any way possible, completing the changeover within 10 minutes becomes possible in the long run, even though it was thought to be impossible to achieve in the first place.

Given that the Toyota System is in place, positive results will remain the outcome as long as continuous improvement efforts are consistently made toward production. It is much better to keep trying in spite of compromising than giving up without even trying due to "unattainable" goals. Our commitment to never compromise and to keep working toward our ideal by continuous improvement efforts, turns impossible goals into possible. In doing so, the adoption of the Toyota System becomes truly meaningful to our production system.

9 Material is poured into metal molds and is pressed into certain shapes.
10 Plastic resin is poured into metal molds to manufacture certain components.
11 Setting up metal molds can easily take up to am hour. However, it can be performed within 10 minutes by the SMED "Single Minute Exchange of Die."
12 Changeover that can be performed while machinery is turned on is called "On-Line Set-Up." On the other hand, changeover that needs to be performed while machinery is turned off is called "Off-Line Set-Up."

Continuous improvement should be based on our changing environment

In recent years, the marketability of electronic appliances averages around 2-3 months, or up to one year in some cases. When a new product is released a set of updated components is necessary and different suppliers are usually chosen to accommodate the change. Production methods also change over time as new technologies become available.

If new components have to be incorporated into assembly, the production method, especially the production line on the shop floor, must be re-examined to ensure productivity. First-time suppliers also need to be persuaded so that Kanbans are accepted in their procurement activities.

In addition, Japanese factories have become much more competitive against Chinese factories than they have against domestic factories. Labor cost of Chinese workers is generally 5 times less than that of Japanese workers. Extending our conventional improvement efforts may not be sufficient to overcome such a huge gap in labor costs. Rather, re-examining and overhauling our entire manufacturing system by carefully formulated continuous improvement strategies is the only effective solution for competing against the Chinese labor market.

Finishing the production of products does not mean that our continuous improvement effort should come to an end. Our continuous improvement efforts toward the production system must be repeated and re-examined according to the changing environment, such as the shortened lifespan of products in general, and the emergence of new competitors, such as Chinese factories.

Continuous improvement is never-ending

As I encountered some footage of Toyota production lines on

TV, I kept wondering how in the world Toyota has always managed to reduce their production costs by 100 billion dollars every year. In fact, Toyota has never (and never will) run out of continuous improvement ideas that are generated from the shop floor.

Toyota is facing more challenges now than it ever has. They need to seek more efficiency in their production systems, as their factories have expanded worldwide and the number of their global workers has increased dramatically in recent years. Such challenges and their continuous improvement efforts are never-ending. Through their never-ending effort, Toyota continues to overcome the challenges associated with the shortened life-cycle of their products. At the same time, Toyota leads the industry by developing various new technologies incorporated into their hybrid vehicles.

Other companies have also incorporated the Toyota System with some promising results. However, their results are never as refined as those achieved by Toyota. These companies must also carry out continuous improvement endlessly to reach the same level of sophistication as Toyota.

THE TOYOTA SYSTEM REQUIRES A TRANSFORMATION OF OUR WAY OF THINKING

So far I have illustrated examples where adoption of the Toyota System was unsuccessful, and the reasons why, in each scenario. Many people, including myself, have made an assumption that the Toyota System can be easily implemented simply by utilizing Kanbans and a Cell Production system. However, as I explained before, continuous improvement, especially changing our perceptions toward manufacturing, must be prioritized on a much higher level prior to incorporating tools such as Kanbans and Cell Production. I repeatedly illustrated that the Toyota System is essentially a flow in production with an average output. A flow can be achieved by one-piece processing that is assisted by standardized production and diligent transportation of items, just like the gentle ripples of a river. A flow is the only way that the Toyota System can be realized with true positive results.

On one hand, some companies still suffer from management crisis even under the Toyota System. One of the main reasons is that the extent of their efforts is limited only to their own factories and the shop floors. Their efforts must be extended beyond their factories so that relationships with suppliers can be greatly improved as well.

The Toyota System is not fundamentally difficult to understand. It is a rather simple concept, however the most difficult challenge is to transform our perceptions that we have toward manufacturing through conventional production systems. It can only be achieved by building our continuous improvement efforts on the shop floor and having a strong leadership from the top management to overcome resistance to new changes.

I strongly think that implementation of the Toyota System is like climbing a mountain. Climbing has become quite popular among mid-aged hobbyists in Japan, but it does not take away the innate risks involved in climbing. No matter how experienced you are, you can still get hurt, or lose your life, if you are not careful enough or underestimate such a dangerous activity.

Climbing requires us to maintain our basic physical strengths (the shop floor's ability to achieve continuous improvement) and proper equipment to be utilized (Kanbans and other tools). Appropriate trails also need to be carefully selected beforehand (methods of promoting the Toyota System). Finally, the mountain peak is reached along with the assistance of a tour guide (consultants) or an experienced team leader who is capable of making the right decisions (the top management). And last but not least, the nature of mountains must be carefully examined by all (the true implications of the Toyota System).

Obviously, nobody is risking his or her own life in the process of adopting the Toyota System. However, without a strong and long-term commitment, we will yield no desirable results and only create confusion and insecurity among the shop floor workers and our suppliers. Merely buying an expensive pair of hiking boots does not lead us to the peak of a mountain. In the same respect, the Toyota System cannot be implemented successfully by depending only on the tools of the Toyota System, such as Kanbans. It can only be accomplished by reforming our perspective and perceptions of manufacturing itself.

As you reach the peak of the mountain, you will certainly discover the presence of an even higher peak—continuous improvement is truly a never-ending journey.

AFTERWORD

OPENING THE BLINDS IN FRONT OF YOUR EYES

It was a short time after I had become involved in the production innovation activities[1] in my own company when I felt like the blinds in front my eyes suddenly lifted up. I will never forget the feeling when I finally understood exactly how Toyota succeeded in reducing inventories and overall production time.

It was when I observed first hand how exactly the quality controls, cost management, and delivery processes were being continuously improved that everything finally made sense in my head. Before this breakthrough I had only been exposed to the principles in literature and never been capable

1 An activity that conducts a comprehensive review of the entire production system to yield substantial results instead of a partial examination of the shop floor. It is often carried out when factories switch over to the Toyota System.

149

of witnessing it in practice.

When I was a college student studying administrative engineering, I conducted much research pertaining to management theories, such as production management, cost management, and quality control. The modern management theories that I had learned in college were supposed to be applied to improving the information and production management systems in my clients' factories when I became a consultant. However, to my surprise, information systems that were based only on theories failed to provide my clients with their desired results and rather caused adverse effects that had to be mitigated. I often became completely lost as to how I could have possibly solved the issues that my clients were facing at the time.

A major turning point occurred in my 15th year as a consultant when I had been placed in charge of supporting the production innovation process of my own company. It focused heavily on my stepping on the shop floor every day and formulating solutions while looking at the actual items in the actual places. This process was a completely innovative and different approach than the conventional approaches that had taken place only in meeting rooms. It allowed me to focus my effort primarily on establishing a total supply-chain management that controlled various sectors in manufacturing such as material suppliers, component manufacturers, assembly manufacturers, purchasing departments and even the end-users. It was not only achieving continuous improvements in individual departments within a factory, but also establishing a flow in the supplier-factory network as a whole. I realized that this was what the Toyota System was all about.

It was when the volume of inventories significantly dropped and the processing time between received orders and delivery was reduced from a few months to only a couple of days, when I felt like the blinds in front of my eyes had lifted. It is quite ironic that the management theories I had learned throughout college and my earlier career failed to lead my clients to effective solutions to their problems. It was the Toyota System, that highly valued the principle of self-discipline among the shop floor workers, that gave me the answers I needed.

After this breakthrough, I continued my consulting efforts to help many clients establish effective production management systems. Since then I have learned that principles of the Toyota System were widely incorporated into their productions, as well as other related management philosophies when I visited their shop floors and talked to the workers face to face. However, according to what I often heard from my clients, their experiences with implementing the Toyota System were not positive and totally different from the successful implementations I had encountered. This book was written to describe such unsuccessful stories.

The Toyota System and Kanban System are widely implemented as though they are the industry standards these days. It has become the requirement for factories to survive in the competitive manufacturing industry. Every factory has a unique approach to adopting the Toyota System with their own strategies and the results vary significantly from positive to negative, as well as no results at all in some cases.

I do not intend to make any judgements as to which implementation methods of the Toyota System are right or wrong. It is totally acceptable for companies to develop their own ways that work the best for realizing their specific needs and goals through the Toyota System.

However, for those who are starting their studies on the Toyota System, I strongly urge them to grasp the true and fundamental implications of the Toyota System principles prior to attempting to implement it in production. By doing so, enough time and discussions can be integrated into formulating the most effective method for each company with the help of this book. That is the very reason why I wrote this book and did not go into too much detail to define every principle or continuous improvement method that supports the Toyota System: to avoid any confusion among new learners. Rather, I wrote this book mainly to show learners the problematic reality behind factories that have tried the Toyota System but ended up bearing various adverse effects. I would like you all to think carefully here as to why these factories have failed, and learn from the common misunderstandings of the Toyota System so that you can formulate your own strategy and prevent the same mistakes from occurring in the first place.

As I was writing this book, I came across a headline that read that Toyota has become the top automobile manufacturer in the world, followed by General Motors of America. It sounded like smooth sailing for Toyota, but the headline did not mean that Toyota had solved all of their challenging problems. Just like the recall cover-up of other auto-makers has recently surfaced to public, Toyota still suffers from, and must strictly administer recalls of, their own products. As an increased number of cars are produced and the components must be standardized to reduce the production cost, their recall issue has had an extensive impact upon their production management and quality controls. Toyota will continue to face many other serious challenges in the future. The quality of their products have become much harder to maintain as many of them are currently manufactured worldwide and innovative technologies, such as those battling the global warming issue, must be continuously developed further to have a competitive edge over other auto makers. Toyota's persistent and effective continuous improvement effort has successfully overcome these challenges and will continue to do so as if there is no end to the horizon.

List of Figures

3. I KNEW THAT KANBANS WERE IMPORTANT

4. CELL PRODUCTION AND KANBANS BECOME MISFORTUNE WITHOUT OVERALL OPTIMIZATION

5. ABSENCE OF PARTICIPATION FROM TOP MANAGEMENT LEADS TO WAR WITHOUT CODES

6. THE TRUE METHODS OF PRACTICING THE TOYOTA SYSTEM

Index

Symbols

5S 11
    and the Toyota System 13
    foundation of 11
    never-ending 15
    principles of 14–15
7 Wastes 12, 14, 126 *See also Waste Elimination*

A

Accounting System 98
    answer to the question on 104
Andon xv
Assembly Lines xvii, 34

Conveyor Belt Production 66–68

D

Daily-use Quantity 47, 49
 decided by production methods 49
Delivery Cycle 47–49, 52
Departments
 accounting 96 *See also Accounting System*
 assembly 92, 112
 business administration 6
 conflicts between 108
 design 94
 inspection 93
 IT 95
 processing 16, 92, 112
 production 93, 95
 purchasing 19, 62, 94
 sales *See also Sales Representative*
  communication with 89
  distrust of factories 87

E

ERP 7–11

F

Factories 4
 and continuous improvement 85
 excuses from 87
 responsibility of inventory 88–89
 spreading improvements to suppliers 79
Factory Management 6
Factory Shop Floor 96 *See also Shop Floor Layout*
Finished Product Inventory 74

L

Labor Cost 100

M

Machinery Changeover Operation xvii
Market Share 2
Mistakes xviii

N

NANAKO 3
Natto 32
Nishimura Machinery 16–18

O

Ohno, Taiichi xvi, 5, 25, 109
One Person Work Cell Production 66
One-Piece Flow 75, 119, 128–130, 134–135
One-Piece Production 76, 130

P

Parts Withdrawal 20, 81 *See also Kanbans*
Planned Manufacturing System 42
Poka-Yoke 38
Post-Process 20, 26, 43
    in Cell Production 77
Preceding Process 20, 26–30, 34, 38
Press Machines 143
Processed Component Inventory 68, 74
Procurement Logistics 81 *See also Transportation*
Production Chief 18
Production Instruction 20, 43 *See also Kanbans*
Production Line Improvement 134

Profits 107
>increasing of 108
>superficial 107

Purchasing Method 79

R

Rate of Production 54, 56
Red Tags 12, 15

S

Sakura Factory 11–12, 15
Sales Representative 85, 96 *See also Departments - Sales*
>communication with factories 89
>distrust of factories 87

Self-Manufacturing 95
Sequential Parts Withdrawal 28, 36, 136
Set in Order 14 *See also 5S*
Set-up Time Improvement 135
Shop Floor Layout 133–134
SMED (Single Minute Exchange of Die) 76, 143
Sorting 14 *See also 5S*
Standardized Components 6
Standardized Operation 135
Standardizing 14 *See also 5S*
Sub-Assembly Lines xvii
Superficial Adaptation 4 *See also Toyota System*
Supermarkets 19–21, 30–32, 138 *See also Just in Time*
>implementing "Just in Time" in 33
>network of stores 34
>operation of 30–32
>sales forecasts of 32

Suppliers 55–61, 79
>co-exist and prosper with the Toyota System 84
>Kanban advantages to 83

U

W

Y

Publications from Enna

From Enna's new classics by Shigeo Shingo to our Lean Origin Series, Enna provides companies with the foundation of knowledge and practical implementation ideas that will ensure your efforts to internalize process improvement. Reach your vision and mission with the expertise within these world-class texts. Call toll-free (866) 249-7348 or visit us on the web at www.enna.com to order or request our free product catalog.

The Toyota Way in Sales and Marketing

Many companies today are trying to implement the ideas and principles of Lean into non-traditional environments, such as service centers, sales organizations and transactional environments. In this book Mr. Ishizaka provides insight on how to apply Lean operational principles and Kaizen to these dynamic and complicated environments.

ISBN 978-1-926537-08-5 | 2009 | $28.99 | Item: 918

Kaizen and the Art of Creative Thinking

Read the book that New York Times Best Selling author of *The Toyota Way*, Jeffrey Liker says, "will help you understand the deep thinking that underlies the real practice of TPS." Dr. Shigeo Shingo's Scientific Thinking Mechanism is the framework from which Toyota and hundreds of other companies have utilized to manage creative problem solving.

ISBN 978-1-897363-59-1 | 2007 | $59.40 | Item: 909

Organizing for Work

When approached from the Lean perspective, H. L. Gantt's *Organizing for Work* provides a window into the American origins of the 2nd Pillar of Lean – Respect for People. Gantt, the creator of Gantt charts, galvanized the human aspect of efficiency with razor sharp clarity. Production improvements go astray because we have "ignored the human factor and failed to take advantage of the ability and desire of the ordinary man to learn and improve his position."

ISBN 978-1-897363-80-5 | 2007 | $59.40 | Item: 910

The Strategos guide to Value Stream & Process Mapping

The Strategos Guide to Value Stream and Process Mapping has proven strategies and helpful tips on facilitating group VSM exercises and puts VSM in the greater Lean context. With photos and examples of related Lean practices, the book focuses on implementing VSM, not just drawing diagrams and graphs.

ISBN 978-1-897363-43-0 | 2007 | $47.00 | Item: 905

The Idea Generator, Quick and Easy Kaizen

The book discusses the Kaizen mind set that enables a company to utilize its resources of the fullest by directly involving all of its manpower in the enhancement and improvement of the productivity of its operations. Published and co-written by Norman Bodek, the Godfather of Lean.

ISBN 978-0-971243-69-9 | 2001 | $47.52 | Item: 902

JIT is Flow

Hirano's *5 Pillars o the Visual Workplace* and *JIT Implementation Manual* were classics. They contained detailed descriptions of techniques and clear instructions. This book highlights the depth of the thought process behind Hirano's work. The clarity which Hirano brings to JIT/Lean and the delineation of the principles involved will be invaluable to every leader and manager aiming for business excellence.

ISBN 978-0-971243-61-3 | 2007 | $47.52 | Item: 903

Training Materials:
JIT Factory Flow Kit

If your company is serious about implementing a Lean Transformation, every person should go through this training. This hands-on simulation demonstrates the effectiveness of Just in Time manufacturing; it shows how much easier job functions can be and how efficient all employees can become if the simple and easy rules of JIT are followed. It is dynamic enough for high-level management training, yet has enough detail for production staff as well; provides the "Ah-ha, I get it!" factor of all your employees. In less than two hours you will have all your staff agreeing to move to a Lean Production System.

ISBN 978-1-897363-60-7 | 2007 | $479.99 | Item: 1081

5S Training Package

Our 5S Solution Packages will help your company create a sustainable 5S program that will turn your shop floor around and put you ahead of the competition. All of the benefits that come from Lean Manufacturing are built upon a strong foundation of 5S. Enna's solution packages will show you how to implement and sustain an environment of continuous improvement.

Version 1: Sort, Straighten, Sweep, Standardize and Sustain

ISBN 978-0-973750-90-4 | 2005 | $429.99 | Item: 12

Version 2: Sort, Set In Order, Shine, Standardize and Sustain

ISBN 978-1-897363-25-6 | 2006 | $429.99 | Item: 17

To Order:

Mail orders and checks to:
Enna Products Corporation
ATTN: Order Processing
1602 Carolina Street, Unit B3
Bellingham, WA 98229
USA
Phone: (866) 249-7348
Fax: (905) 481-0756
Email: info@enna.com

We accept checks and all major credit cards.

Notice:
All prices are in US Dollars and are subject to change without notice.

Breinigsville, PA USA
18 February 2010
232728BV00002B/1/P